"Classical Latin Creatively Taught"

Latin for Children

Primer B

Activity Book!

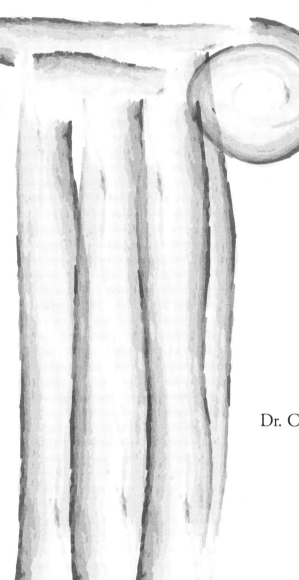

Robby Baddorf
Dr. Christopher Perrin

Latin for Children: Primer B • *Activity Book!*
© Classical Academic Press, 2005
Version 2.2

Classical Academic Press
2151 Market Street
Camp Hill, PA 17011

www.ClassicalAcademicPress.com

ISBN: 978-1-60051-011-3

Illustrations & cover by:
Robby Baddorf

Parents & Teachers:

This book was intended as a learing-aid to students studying Latin from the **Latin For Children: Primer B** text-book. It follows that text-book chapter for chapter. Thus, the vocabulary words learned on chapter seven of the text-book correlate to those in chapter seven of this activity book.

Not all puzzles will appeal to all students. Feel free to have students jump around or even skip puzzles. Our goal is not to stump the students with "impossible" puzzles, rather, with a reasonable sense of challenge, have students continue practicing their Latin in a setting that is fun, playful and full of games.

Ideas:

Use highlighters for the word search puzzles. This should help minimize the muddle of circles.

Use colored pencils on the matching games to delineate one line from another.

Encourage students to work together (when available) on the more challenging puzzles.

Have students create their own puzzles and games to share with others!

Look. Look Again!
4 games in 1

Don't forget the group
game, at the back of
the book!

chapter 1

Instructions:
You need instructions?!

THE START OF A BEAUTIFUL FRIENDSHIP!

Across
1. equipped
2. outermost
3. I approve
5. I think
7. next
9. I pray
11. to think
13. to expect
15. expected
17. dead
20. I equipped
21. living
22. living
23. approve
25. outermost
26. I thought
27. to approve

Down
1. I equip
2. I expect
3. last
4. to equip
5. next
6. I expected
7. next
8. prayed
10. last
11. thought
12. outermost
14. I approved
16. dead
18. dead
19. last
21. living
24. to pray

Welcome back, those of you who puzzled your whole way through *Latin For Children, Primer A Activity Book!* And those that missed that ticket out of Casablanca--just wait & see what fun awaits you!

A TOUCH-UP JOB

We were trying to put a little paint on things around here to clean 'em up, and well,... some white paint spilled. Can you help us clean up this chart?

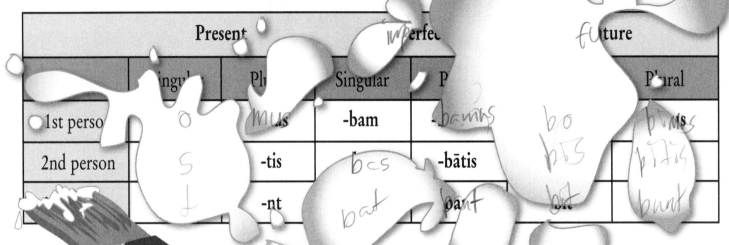

	Present		Imperfect		future	
	Singular	Plural	Singular	Plural		Plural
1st person	o	-mus	-bam	-bamus	bo	bimus
2nd person	s	-tis	bcs	-bātis	bcs	bītis
3rd person	t	-nt	bat	bant	bit	bunt

CODE BREAKERS

Circle the correct boxes to crack the code!

PROBĀTIS

Present	Imperfect	Future
Singular		Plural
1st Person	2nd Person	3rd Person

PROBĀBUNT

Present	Imperfect	Future
Singular		Plural
1st Person	2nd Person	3rd Person

ORĀNT

Present	Imperfect	Future
Singular		Plural
1st Person	2nd Person	3rd Person

PUTĀBĀMUS

Present	Imperfect	Future
Singular		Plural
1st Person	2nd Person	3rd Person

EXSPECTĀBIT

Present	Imperfect	Future
Singular		Plural
1st Person	2nd Person	3rd Person

Hide 'n Seek

Yeah, all those pesky little Latin words are playing around again and well, Mom just called "dinner time." Can you run around the apple orchard, translating the English words and finding the Latin before any of 'em get in trouble for being late?

```
E P M X G O I A A E E K W
O X O H Z X F F Z X X A Q
T D S S Q Y T R M T S F Z
G H L P T J U U V R P P O
P R V Z E R W I A E E O R
I R F I Y C E T N M C S N
W B O K P Q T M A U T T Ā
P P Z B S V D Ā U S Ā R V
U D O R Ā T U M T S R E Ī
T J C S T B A M U E M Y
Ā M O R T U U M O G M U R
T P U T Ō R K M R K M M Q
U U P A X S E C T B I T B
M V Ī V U S X M U E T W Y
P O S T E R U M A X C C M
F Y W N M V K V W T W Z Z
X N B U P M Ī K N R I R X
D(P U T Ā R E)V R E J O A
E X S P E C T Ō A M R S W
E X T R E M U M J A A N E
Y H Q Z V O O U A R Q H D
U B Q G C R J R H Y M C N
A B J P F Ō V F N D K W G
X S J Y O R Ā R E Ā Q I K
O V T E B S Z S O N R C A
E X S P E C T Ā V Ī P E M
O S P V U O W E U D O H O
O R U R Ī T R F R M S P R
R A Ā O O V Ā N P A T B T
N R S V W B U V Ā C E C U
Ō C E D Ī Q Ā M Ī T R V U
P R O B Ā R E V E T U A S
P C K I S V D U Ī Q S M M
R W M E L U Q F C R S V Q
O Y J V A Y G T X Q J B G
B H R O U S R F A J O A K
Ō F M E N I Y P Z B T P D
```

_____, I pray

_____, to pray

_____, I prayed

_____, prayed

_____, I equip

_____, to equip

_____, I equipped

_____, equipped

_____, I expect

_____, to expect

_____, I expected

_____, expected

_____, I think

_____, to think

_____, I thought

_____, thought

_____, I approve

_____, to approve

_____, I approved

_____, approved

_____, living

_____, living

_____, living

_____, dead

_____, dead

_____, dead

_____, next

_____, next

_____, next

_____, last

_____, last

_____, last

_____, outermost

_____, outermost

_____, outermost

Did you know?

Ticket!

Ad idem
"Of the same mind"

3

Wall Flowering

amat

Hank doesn't really know that many people, and... he's sorta shy.
Can you help him (Mr. Singular) connect with the Latin words (by drawing
connecting lines)? Since you're such a good match-maker, why not try
matching up the plural words as well.

videō

amant

videt

vident

amas

amātis

vidēmus

vides

amāmus

amō

vidētis

Plural

Singular

Ever win a gold-fish before? Golly, here's your chance! Connect the correct ping-pong balls to the correct bowls & you win!

A Little Fishy!

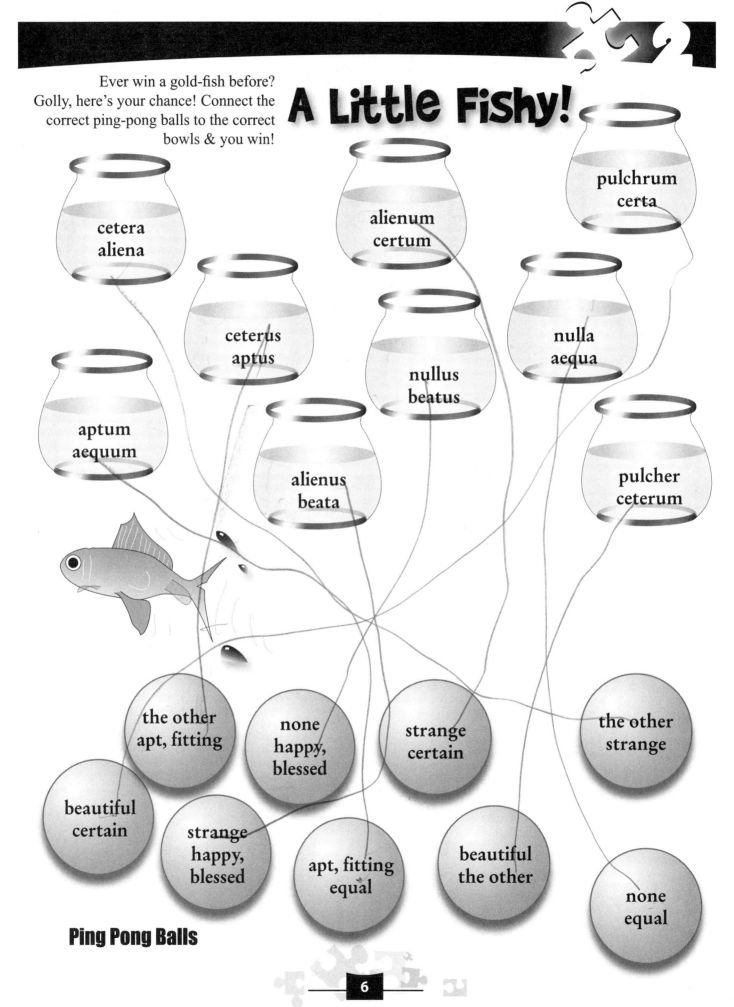

cetera aliena

alienum certum

pulchrum certa

ceterus aptus

nulla aequa

nullus beatus

aptum aequum

alienus beata

pulcher ceterum

the other apt, fitting

none happy, blessed

strange certain

the other strange

beautiful certain

strange happy, blessed

apt, fitting equal

beautiful the other

none equal

Ping Pong Balls

chapter 3

All aboard!

Across
3. injury, injustice
6. number, measure
8. nature, birth
9. star
10. measure, mode
11. care
12. measure, mode
13. nature, birth

Down
1. number, measure
2. cause
4. injury, injustice
5. care
7. star
11. cause

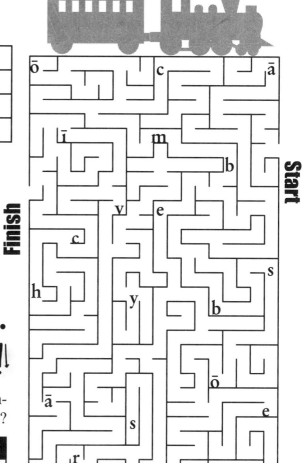

MINI MAZER!

Can you collect the letters that you find, in order, from beginning to end, and find out what the hidden review word is?

1st	2nd	3rd	4th	5th	6th

English Translation:_____

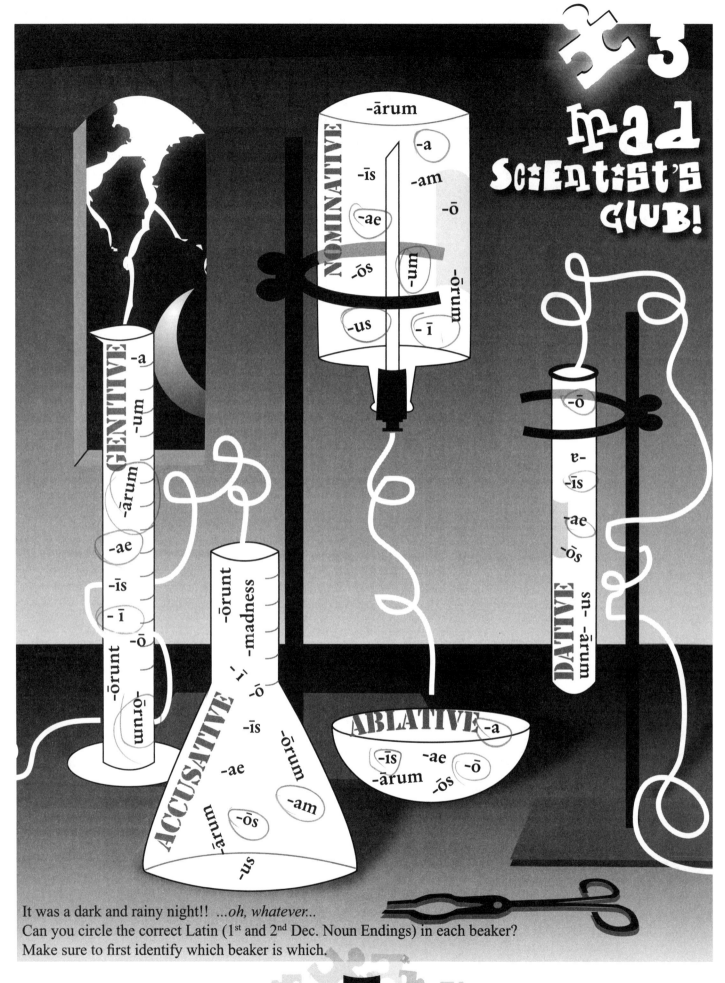

It was a dark and rainy night!! ...*oh, whatever...*
Can you circle the correct Latin (1st and 2nd Dec. Noun Endings) in each beaker?
Make sure to first identify which beaker is which.

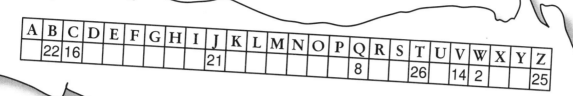

A	B	C	D	E	F	G	H	I	J	K	L	M	N	O	P	Q	R	S	T	U	V	W	X	Y	Z
22	16								21						8			26		14	2			25	

AGENT 4¼

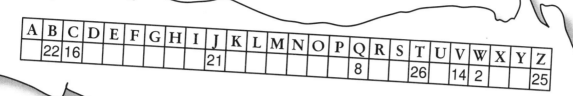

TOP SECRET

Coded message

Ō , 24 5 13 18 6
20 13

Ā T Ū , T , B T
23 26 13 18 , 23 18 26 7 13 17 , 22 24 13 26 9

Ō , Q
20 13 23 , 24 , 17 8 7 24 5

C , C
16 18 7 19 18 , 16 18 7 19 17

B Ā , T V
5 13 20 22 13 17 , 26 20 18 5 5 13 20 14 17

V Ī V , V
14 14 7 19 , 11 24 14 24 23 10

T ,
15 20 13 26 7 7 19 , 3 17 18 3

T , T
5 20 19 26 17 13 18 , 23 17 12 26

C Ū , C
16 13 18 , 16 18 13 17

T , T
17 12 26 13 17 15 7 15 , 20 7 26 17 13 15 20 19 26

C T , - C T
16 17 13 26 7 19 , 16 17 13 26 18 24 23

T , T
19 26 17 11 11 18 17 , 19 26 18 13

C , B T
5 7 11 16 9 17 13 , 22 17 18 7 26 24 4 7 11

T , T
18 11 24 17 23 7 19 , 19 26 13 18 23 10 17

Ī , B ,
23 7 15 17 13 , 23 7 15 22 17 13 , 15 17 18 19 7 13 17
23 7 15 17 13

HINT: You might try this one first rather than next. →

Sorry, all the good agent numbers were taken. Anyway... we need you to cipher these coded words. They're Latin words with their English translations but there is more here then just this week's words. Can you figure it out, Agent 4¼?

chapter 4

LFC screwy tales

You've seen these before haven't you? They're crazy! They're fun! ***They're crazy fun!*** Here's how it works in case you don't know:

You can play this game alone, or better yet, with a friend who is learning Latin as well. Go through the story picking words from the list of Latin nouns, verbs & adjectives from the list provided (or from your own memory of *LFC Primer A* and/or *LFC Primer B*). Only when you're done filling in all the spaces with the English translations, go back and read your story out loud from the beginning. Use pencil and try it again with all new words if you want. Enjoy!

Oh... and don't forget to laugh!

The Princess and the Pea

Once upon a time, amidst a terrible and _____ night, a lone girl, dripping
                                              adjective

_____ & _____s, straggled up to the castle door and _____
    noun   noun   verb

loudly. The Prince answered the door. He wasn't sure he should let the _____
                                                                              adjective

girl inside, but she claimed to be a _____. Wanting to test her, the prince put
                                          noun

a _____ little pea under 40 mattresses. The lone girl tried to _____
      adjective   verb

all night but simply couldn't. The next morning, the Prince asked the lone girl how she

_____. "Terribly!" she said. "It felt like I was sleeping on a _____
      verb   adjective

_____ all night long!" The End.
    noun

List of Nouns, Verbs & Adjectives ⟶

VERBS	NOUNS	ADJEC.
administrō	aedificium	altus
absum	animus	argentum
amō	aquae	bonus
audeō	astrum	clarus
cantō	caelum	defessus
caveō	capillus	dignus
cēno	casa	dubius
clamō	cēna	dūrus
cogitō	collum	falsus
interrogō	dea	horrendus
consilium	deus	ignavus
creō	donum	īratus
doleō	epistula	iustus
errō	equus	iuxtā
explorō	fēmina	laetus
flō	fenestra	longus
laborō	ferrum	magnus
moneō	ferus	malus
nāvigō	filia	minimus
nominō	filius	mirus
oppugnō	fluvius	miser
pugnō	folium	novus
rogō	fossa	parātus
spectō	germana	parvus
agitō	germanus	pessimus
stō	hortus	plēnus
teneō	humus	proximus
imperō	insula	pūrus
velum	lupus	rectus
videō	magister	serēnus
vigilō	magistra	sordidus
vitō	mēnsa	tacitus
vocō	mūrus	ultimus
orō	pabulum	varius
putō	pagina	vīvus
	poeta	mortuus
	puella	postremus
	puer	extremus
	rēgīna	pulcher
	saxum	alienus
	sepulchrum	beatus
	silva	medius
	vallum	
	ventus	
	vir	
	stella	
	vīnum	

Robin Hood

Greetings Latin adventurer! We need someone to venture into Sherwood forest and find the poor Latin words that have strayed from the path. Can you find all 3?

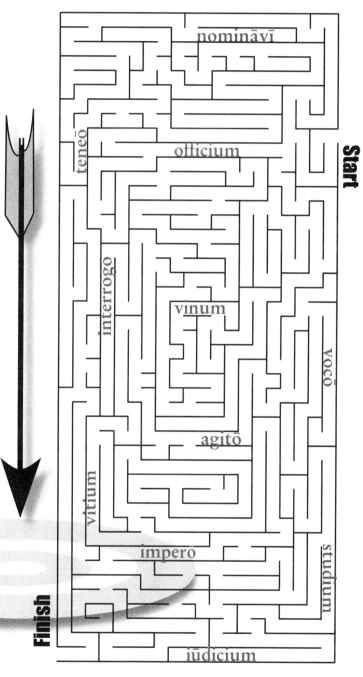

Found & Translated:

_____, _____

_____, _____

_____, _____

You'll need to load the correct spaceships with the correct Latin (Irregular Verb: Sum, esse) in order for there to be a **blast-off**! *Can you do it space cadet?!*

mission to mars

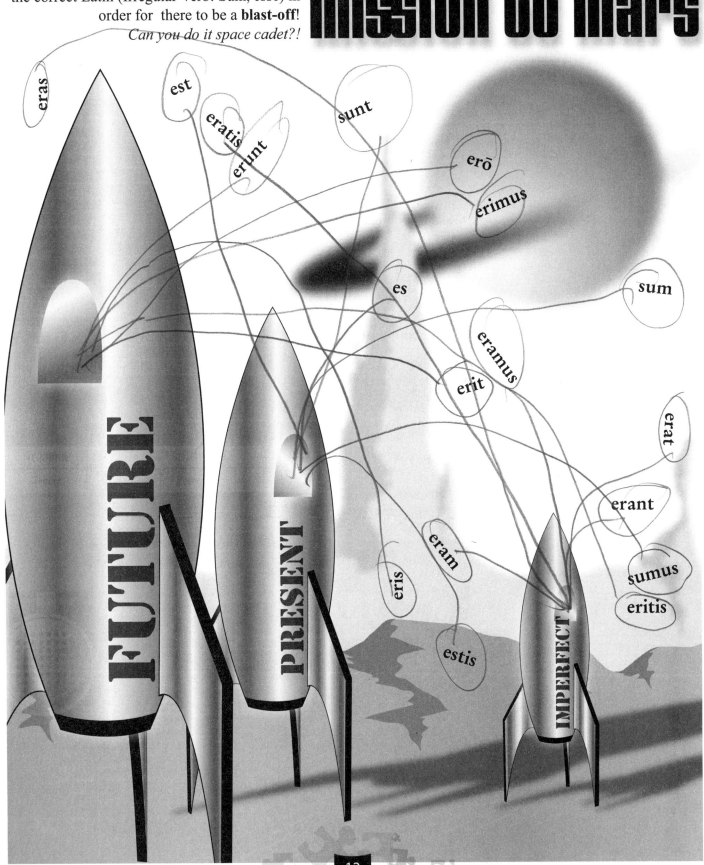

REVIEW 5

Across

1. duty, respect
3. to name, mention, call by name
8. outermost
10. to order or command
11. to expect
12. last
13. I approve
14. to help or manage
16. cause
17. apt, fitting
20. prayed
21. trial, legal investigation
23. approved
26. I pray
27. last
28. living
29. happy, blessed
30. dead
31. none
32. to think
33. trial, legal investigation
34. number, measure
37. to drive, stir up, agitate
38. number, measure
40. apt, fitting
42. strange
44. star
47. measure, mode
48. strange
50. the other

52. cause
53. to drive, stir up, agitate
55. star
56. none
57. injury, injustice
58. care
60. nature, birth
61. the other
62. zeal, study
63. to help or manage
64. to name, mention, call by name
66. apt, fitting
68. I thought
71. to equip
72. outermost
74. care
76. duty, respect
78. none

79. I expected
80. I equipped
81. last
82. to order or command
83. middle
84. to help or manage
85. I expect
86. measure, mode
87. to help or manage
88. zeal, study

KING OF THE GARGANUAN!

EEEK!

ACK!

Whatever you do, don't look on the next page!

NOTE: the puzzle overlaps from page to page

SCREEEAM!

OH MY!

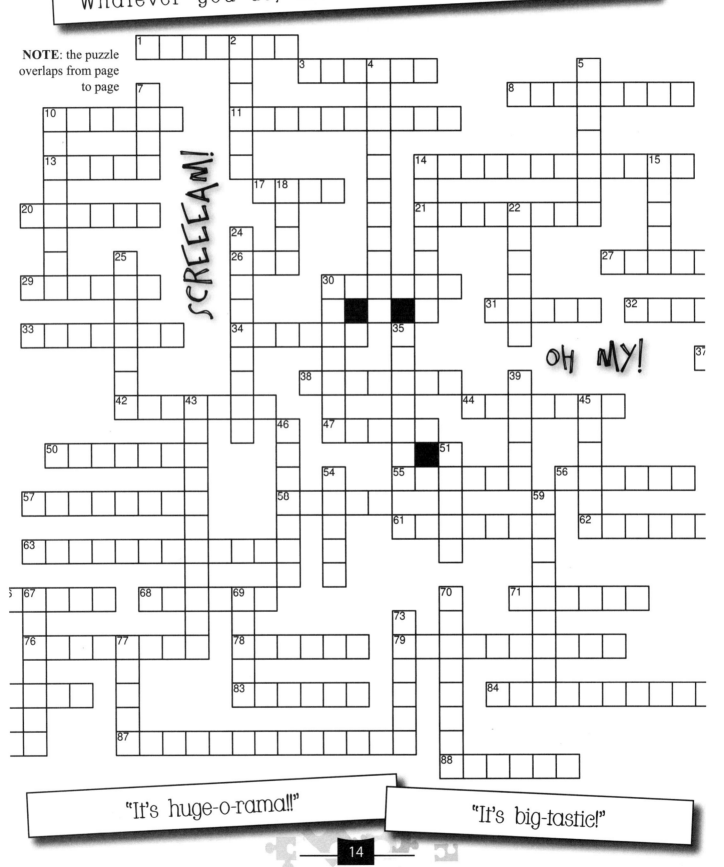

"It's huge-o-rama!!"

"It's big-tastic!"

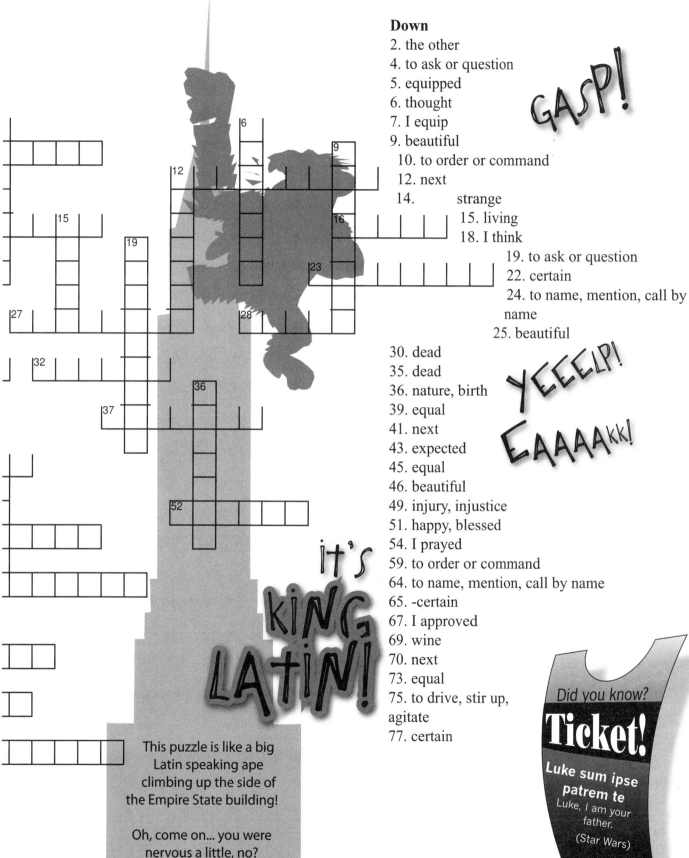

Down

2. the other
4. to ask or question
5. equipped
6. thought
7. I equip
9. beautiful
10. to order or command
12. next
14. strange
15. living
18. I think
19. to ask or question
22. certain
24. to name, mention, call by name
25. beautiful
30. dead
35. dead
36. nature, birth
39. equal
41. next
43. expected
45. equal
46. beautiful
49. injury, injustice
51. happy, blessed
54. I prayed
59. to order or command
64. to name, mention, call by name
65. -certain
67. I approved
69. wine
70. next
73. equal
75. to drive, stir up, agitate
77. certain

GASP!

YEEELP!

EAAAAKK!

it's KING LATIN!

This puzzle is like a big Latin speaking ape climbing up the side of the Empire State building!

Oh, come on... you were nervous a little, no?

Did you know?

Ticket!

Luke sum ipse patrem te
Luke, I am your father.
(Star Wars)

chapter 6

Latin MP3

Someone just came home with this strange Latin-chanting gizmo and we can't get it to play. Technology—I tell ya! Can you draw the correct ear-bud wire (dots, dashes, wavy) next to the parts of is, ea, id? Draw all the wires that match (there might be more than one wire per Latin word). We've got one working already.

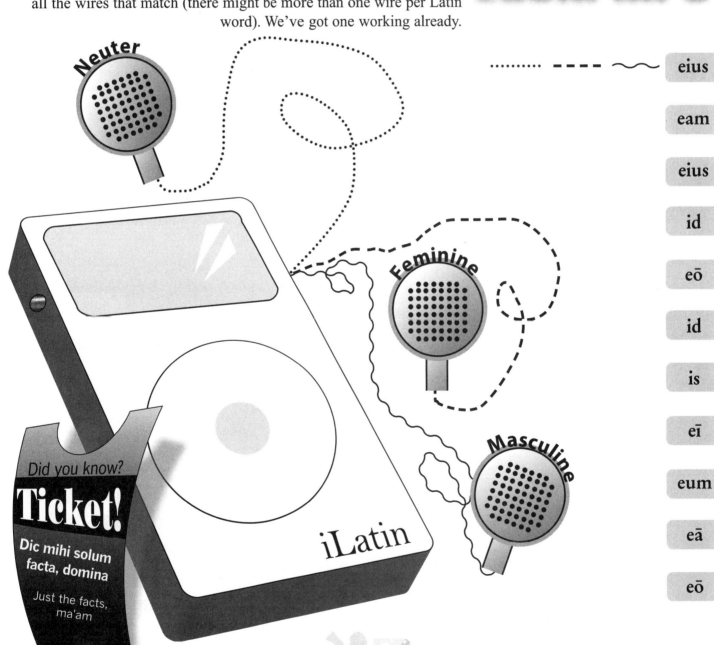

Neuter

Feminine

Masculine

Did you know?

Ticket!

Dic mihi solum facta, domina

Just the facts, ma'am

iLatin

eius
eam
eius
id
eō
id
is
eī
eum
eā
eō

Word Crossing

Down
1. flame
2. her (accusative case)
4. flame
5. hour
6. tongue, language

Across
3. tear
4. shape, beauty
6. tear
7. him (accusative case)
8. door
10. thanks
11. tongue, language
14. hour

Down Cont.
8. it (nominative or accusative case)
9. shape, beauty
12. door
13. thanks

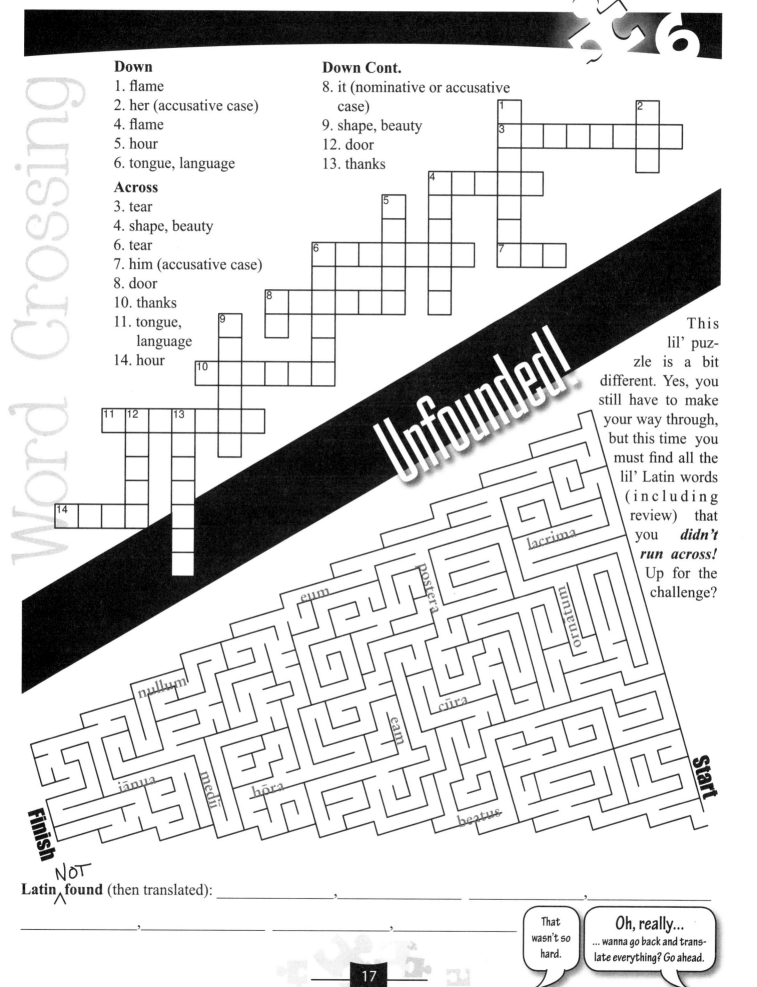

Unfounded!

This lil' puzzle is a bit different. Yes, you still have to make your way through, but this time you must find all the lil' Latin words (including review) that you ***didn't run across!*** Up for the challenge?

lacrima
postera
eum
ornatum
nullum
cūra
eam
iānua
mediī
hōra
beatus

Start

Finish

Latin NOT **found** (then translated): _____,_____ _____,

_____,_____ _____,_____

That wasn't so hard.

Oh, really... ... wanna go back and translate everything? Go ahead.

TALL TALE

Oh boy! It's story time.
We're gonna need some help in translating this simple story that uses personal pronouns. It's a real tear-jerker. And like one of those Shakespeare tragedies, everyone kicks the—
                    Oh, we'll just let you read it.

Femina casam ornat.

Filia eius casam pulchram videt.

"Casa pulchra est!" filia clamat.

Filius eius dicit quoque,
"Ea pulchra est!"

Femina ambulat ad eum et dicit,
"Multas gratias ago tibi."

Filia tristis (sad) est. Femina videt filiam et lacrimas eius.

Femina ambulat ad eam et dicit,
"Multas gratias ago etiam (also) tibi."

Nunc (now) filia laetus est. Ea dicit,
"Amo te mater!"

chapter 7

PUZZLE ME THIS

ŪLAN, OMNO

⬚⬚⬚⬚⬚ , ⬚⬚⬚⬚
11

REOIAMM, YMMERO

⬚⬚⬚⬚⬚⬚ , ⬚⬚⬚⬚⬚⬚
10

NŪALE, NMOO

⬚⬚⬚⬚⬚ , ⬚⬚⬚⬚

XAULŪRI, UYLXUR, EATXVNARCGAE

⬚⬚⬚⬚⬚⬚ , ⬚⬚⬚⬚⬚⬚ , ⬚⬚⬚⬚⬚⬚⬚⬚⬚⬚⬚
9

EAGLĪT, UYETDP, NUTELTAENI

⬚⬚⬚⬚⬚⬚ , ⬚⬚⬚⬚⬚⬚ , ⬚⬚⬚⬚⬚⬚⬚⬚⬚⬚
8

RMOAIEM, EMROYM

⬚⬚⬚⬚⬚⬚ , ⬚⬚⬚⬚⬚⬚

TTAILEER, ETELTR

⬚⬚⬚⬚⬚⬚⬚ , ⬚⬚⬚⬚⬚⬚
2

ERPAO, FRFTOE, RCEISSVE

⬚⬚⬚⬚⬚ , ⬚⬚⬚⬚⬚⬚ , ⬚⬚⬚⬚⬚⬚⬚
3

ĪLOUC, EEY

⬚⬚⬚⬚⬚ , ⬚⬚⬚
5

ORPAEE, TFFOER, EREICSVS

⬚⬚⬚⬚⬚⬚ , ⬚⬚⬚⬚⬚⬚ , ⬚⬚⬚⬚⬚⬚⬚⬚
4

ILTRETA, ERLTTE

⬚⬚⬚⬚⬚⬚⬚ , ⬚⬚⬚⬚⬚⬚
6

LSEAGTU, TEDPYU, ATUENTLENI

⬚⬚⬚⬚⬚⬚⬚ , ⬚⬚⬚⬚⬚⬚ , ⬚⬚⬚⬚⬚⬚⬚⬚⬚⬚
1

RIALUXEŪ, XURUYL, EAEATNVRGCXA

⬚⬚⬚⬚⬚⬚⬚⬚ , ⬚⬚⬚⬚⬚⬚ , ⬚⬚⬚⬚⬚⬚⬚⬚⬚⬚⬚
7

UUOCSL, YEE

⬚⬚⬚⬚⬚⬚ , ⬚⬚⬚

Can you unshuffle this week's vocabulary words (both Latin and English) and find the code phrase located in the code box?

CODE BOX

! 11 10 9 8 7

6 5 4

h 3 2 1

Coffee-Shop Cork-Board

I was in ordering my double mocha Swiss-Chai decaf latte and I happened to notice these odd Latin cards on the bulletin board. Looks like these Plural Personal Pronouns need a little help? Up for the puzzle?

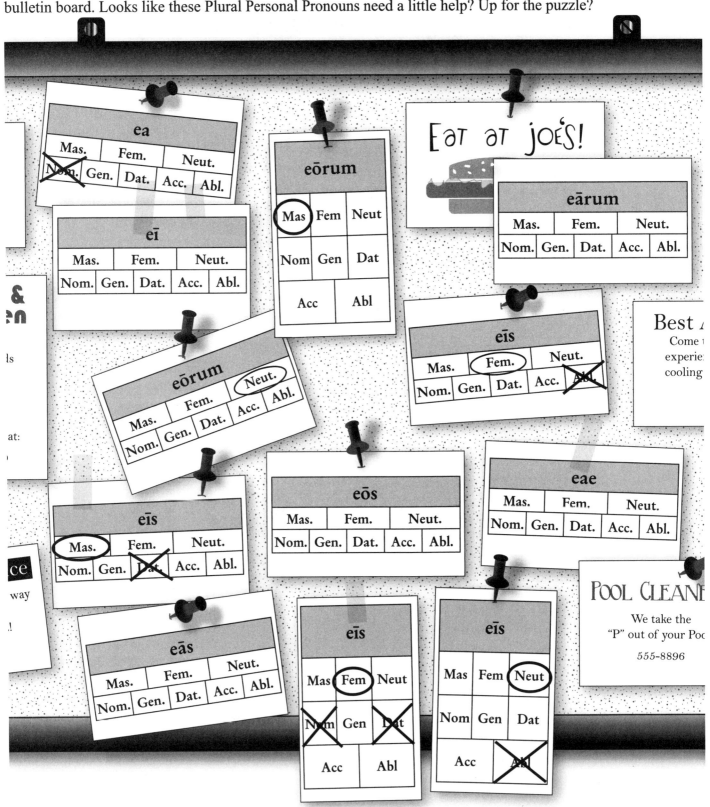

Dear Great Aunt Loise,

I am writting you this *epistula,* and hope that it finds you very *beatus* . I wanted to offer you *gratia* for the *mira cena* you offered my *amicam* and I the other evening when the *stellae* were out and the *pulchra luna* was quite *magna.*

I enjoyed our talk around the *mensa* even though Alice secretly thought it was *miser.* I really didn't know that at one point you were a *nauta* adventuring on the open *mare* with the *ventō* in your hair. And the time you killed *octō lupī* with your *nudīs manibus.* Is it really true that you jumped through a *fenestram* and rode a *ferum equum* while you were nearly *caecus?* What a *fabula*! You caused me *cogitāre* when you told us about the *sordida ianua ferri*

that you had to open every day for school--and uphill both ways at that! It was your tale about climbing that tall *montem* and your nearly freezing to *mortem* that surprised me the most. And I thought you just did needle point!

Amor and kisses.

chapter 8

OK-CORAL!

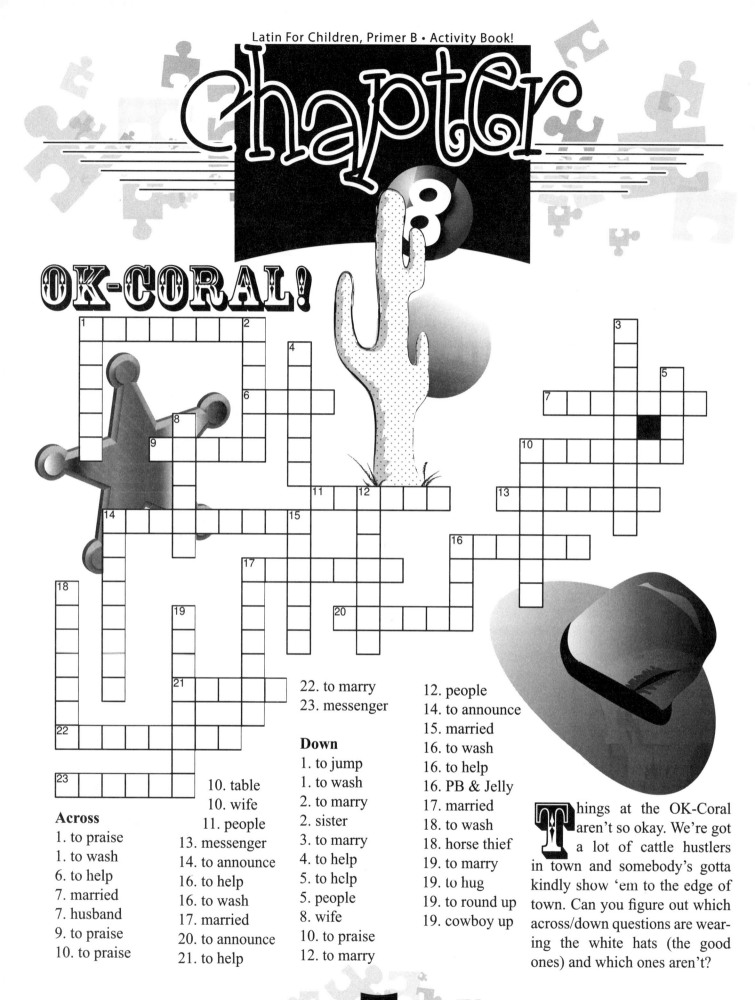

22. to marry
23. messenger

Down
1. to jump
1. to wash
2. to marry
2. sister
3. to marry
4. to help
5. to help
5. people
8. wife
10. to praise
12. to marry

10. table
10. wife
11. people
13. messenger
14. to announce
16. to help
16. to wash
17. married
20. to announce
21. to help

12. people
14. to announce
15. married
16. to wash
16. to help
16. PB & Jelly
17. married
18. to wash
18. horse thief
19. to marry
19. to hug
19. to round up
19. cowboy up

Across
1. to praise
1. to wash
6. to help
7. married
7. husband
9. to praise
10. to praise

Things at the OK-Coral aren't so okay. We're got a lot of cattle hustlers in town and somebody's gotta kindly show 'em to the edge of town. Can you figure out which across/down questions are wearing the white hats (the good ones) and which ones aren't?

MESSY

I was making myself some breakfast when someone yelled, "Leggo my ego," ...so I did. Now we've got this big mess on the floor to clean up. Can some chap or chapette (is that a word?) help us clean it all up? Can you suck up the 1st Person Personal Pronouns in the correct vacuums?

nōs

mē

ego

meī

nostrum, nostrī

nōbīs

nōs

nōbīs

mihi

Singular

HOOPER

Plural

Did you know?

Ticket!

In totidem verbis

In so many words

WATER RESCUE!

8

A big transport ship went down in the storm last night. Fortunately no one was hurt but can you pilot the helicopter (with one continuously drawn line) and circle around the correct Latin pairs left adrift?

exspectātum
I think

iūdiciī
trial, legal
investigation

hōra
shape,
beauty

opera
effort,
services

administrō
to order
or command

laudātum
to praise

iniūrīa
nature,
birth

maritō
to marry

legatus
effort,
services

causa
cause

maritus,
to announce

aequum,
equal

lacrima
tear

Can you translate then find?
Yeah, alllll of them.

```
K G W L T A C P X V E J Q S E V M O D X N S B N C
Y N R Y T V O S R W C J V D A U B W Z S C L H T G
I S P U X O V Z S O C S E O I C P U S F C Q D C E
M N M U O C Q E O Y E X M S O A C U C E X J B V B
A D I U V Ō O L Q K E L N C F D P U G R E M Ī W L
M G X Q I Q W N P Q Z A I P B O R M L N X K D X S
P U G N A C A T W P O R Y Ī Z P G T A Ī A V W Z P
W X P A Y J U C G I H E N Z M T Z E K M L E R K C
S O T R I T R I H W K M B L Q Ā R Q T W S Q A L T
I C R M Q G W S M B V U G C W T S M Y I S T V F O
Z E M Ō O B D H I I V S P A P U G A Ō D C L O A Q
H W T R R S F G A Q W G R D G M M C A T V N C Q Y
O Y F U J I T O E N N I O O M V I H O M U B Ā M K
K U N M B O D H N B M Z E L N M Z Q M E Ō M R L U
U N W K M A Z L R U W P L Z P K J Y M W W T E T I
X L I B E L L U M W M A I A P Z N D A Y I U U F I
P X D V P Z H M I S G F U D N H K L F O Y A A M R
S G O N Y F T Z V E D A M O I Y B Y R W W C V O H
M A Z P G Q M T L V U S W P H G U J U C R Y V Y K
C K C F A D I U T U M B W T F C M K W O C B V E A
A V O C Ā V Ī M W V E D E Ō I M B Q M K P A Z N A
A W F T U S U U S R X Q G L Z Ō G X O R Q Q C I D
A D I R J L G L A D I U S A L V Y A L V H X M Y O
O A I T B R U U H K V F I R M Ī I G A N Z G S O K
G Q W U G R P S N F O D T G K O V X G E A L K W I
D D B F V R J G C R O F R S J A V C I E D A A H R
R Z L L U Ī T A A F O D Z U U A R Ē W V O D F M V
C M Z Y K U N A D I U V Ā R E A M M R B P I X C K
A V O C Ā T U M I P R T C C C A D O A E T Ī V N H
N L S Y G S T C X G Q G M L H E E O V I Ā Z G O P
T U M U L Ī D G O V S T O S Q Y O A P Ī V X R T K
A U I I R Y T Q H R Y U V P R P F K E T Ī M X V U
M O V E Ō D I K R A Q W Ē L N Y V B L C Ā Y J U K
F F Q Y N Q A M O V E Ō R K V P L F Y X Y R R S C
A W K O G K J H P A T W E C E J V X D X H K E A F
```

_____ help, aid
_____ help, aid
_____ help, aid
_____ help, aid
_____ select, adopt
_____ select, adopt
_____ select, adopt
_____ select, adopt
_____ move away
_____ move away
_____ move away
_____ move away
_____ call away
_____ call away
_____ call away
_____ call away
_____ move
_____ move
_____ move
_____ move
_____ oar
_____ oar
_____ little bag
_____ little bag
_____ hill, mound
_____ hill, mound
_____ fight
_____ fight
_____ sword
_____ sword
_____ war, battle
_____ war, battle
_____ battle
_____ battle
_____ arms, weapons
_____ arms, weapons
(plural only)

Jungle Juice

RAIN WATER COLLECTOR

We've been collecting rain water for days now. Can you help it trickle down through the pipes and filter through the Latin stations in order to obtain clean drinkable water? Fill in the 2nd Person Personal Pronouns Latin stations as you go.

Gen.
Sing.
tuī

Dat.
Plural

Abl.
Sing.

Dat.
Sing.

Nom.
Sing.

Nom.
Plural

Abl.
Plural

Gen.
Plural

Acc.
Sing.

Acc.
Plural

WIGGLE WAGGLE

Can you start at the start and end at the end? Oh, and translate as you go.

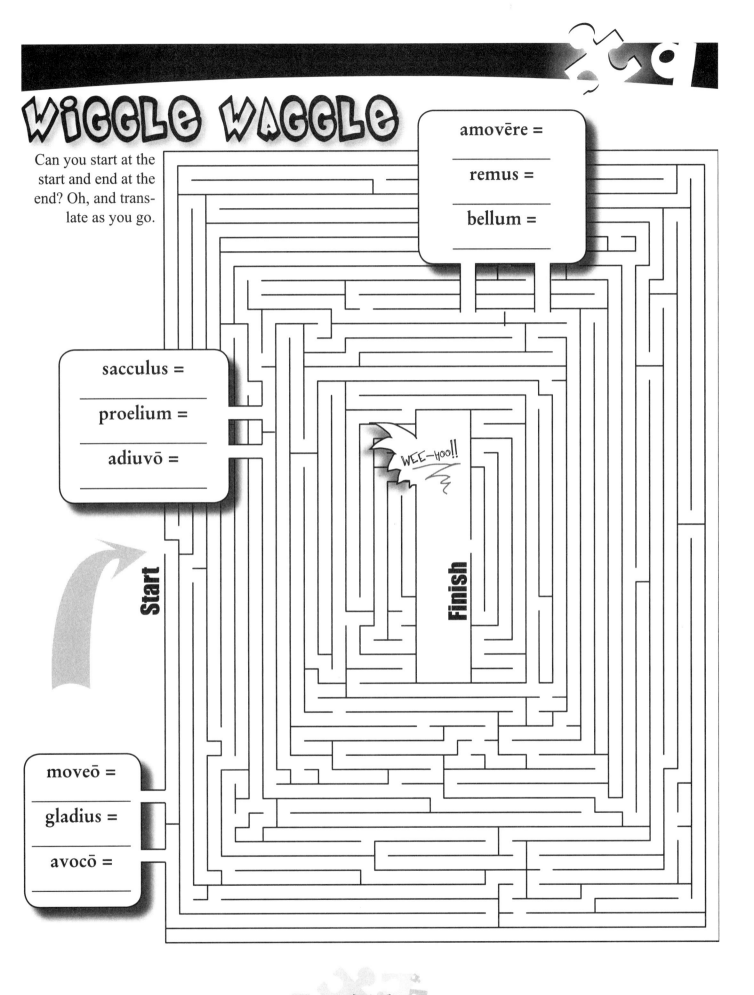

amovēre = _____

remus = _____

bellum = _____

sacculus = _____

proelium = _____

adiuvō = _____

Start

Finish

WEE-HOO!!

moveō = _____

gladius = _____

avocō = _____

chapter

REVIEW 10

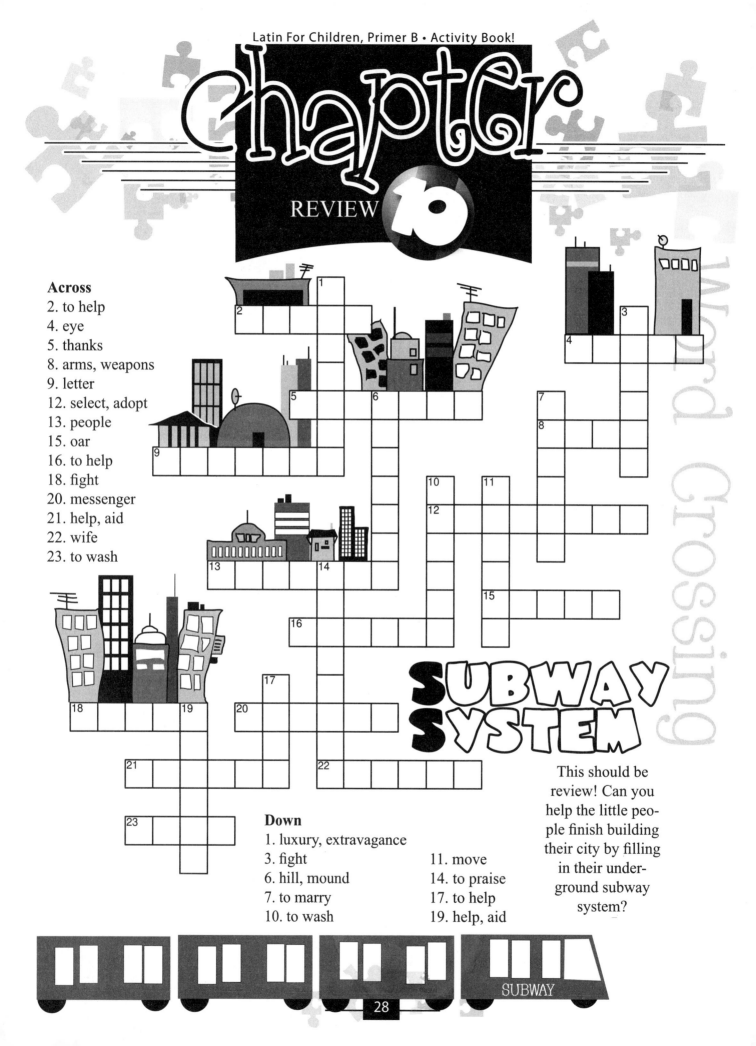

Word Crossing

Across
2. to help
4. eye
5. thanks
8. arms, weapons
9. letter
12. select, adopt
13. people
15. oar
16. to help
18. fight
20. messenger
21. help, aid
22. wife
23. to wash

Down
1. luxury, extravagance
3. fight
6. hill, mound
7. to marry
10. to wash
11. move
14. to praise
17. to help
19. help, aid

This should be review! Can you help the little people finish building their city by filling in their underground subway system?

SUBWAY SYSTEM

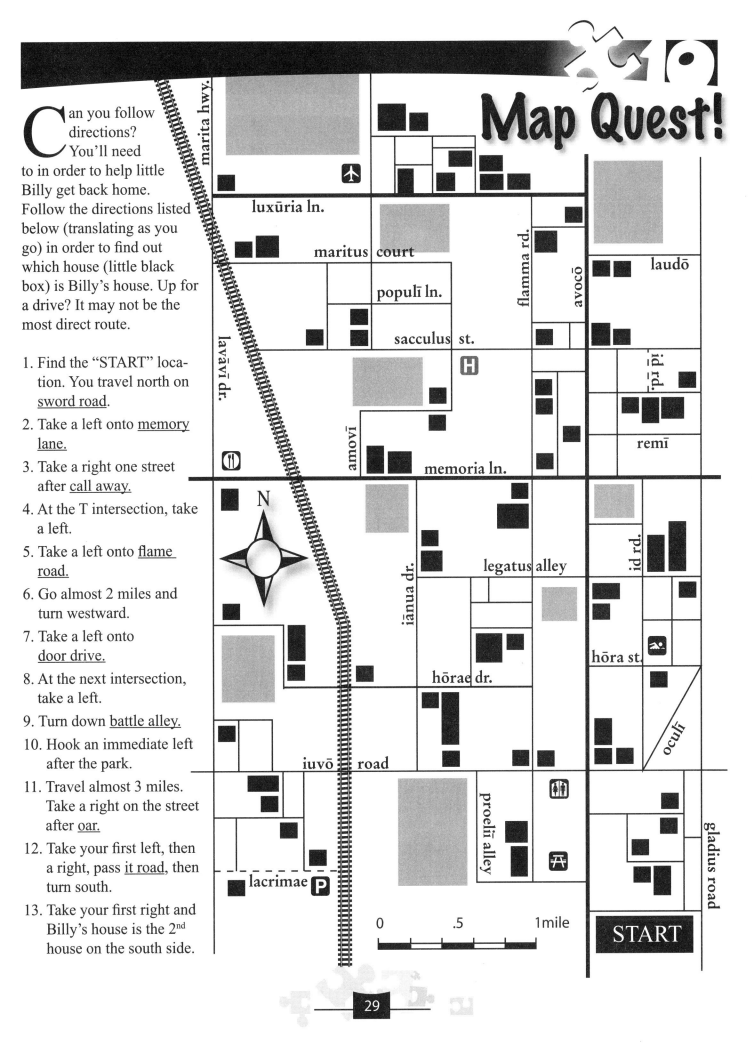

Map Quest!

Can you follow directions? You'll need to in order to help little Billy get back home. Follow the directions listed below (translating as you go) in order to find out which house (little black box) is Billy's house. Up for a drive? It may not be the most direct route.

1. Find the "START" location. You travel north on <u>sword road</u>.

2. Take a left onto <u>memory lane.</u>

3. Take a right one street after <u>call away.</u>

4. At the T intersection, take a left.

5. Take a left onto <u>flame road.</u>

6. Go almost 2 miles and turn westward.

7. Take a left onto <u>door drive.</u>

8. At the next intersection, take a left.

9. Turn down <u>battle alley.</u>

10. Hook an immediate left after the park.

11. Travel almost 3 miles. Take a right on the street after <u>oar.</u>

12. Take your first left, then a right, pass <u>it road</u>, then turn south.

13. Take your first right and Billy's house is the 2nd house on the south side.

Another Shot

Go ahead. Take another crack at the review vocab!

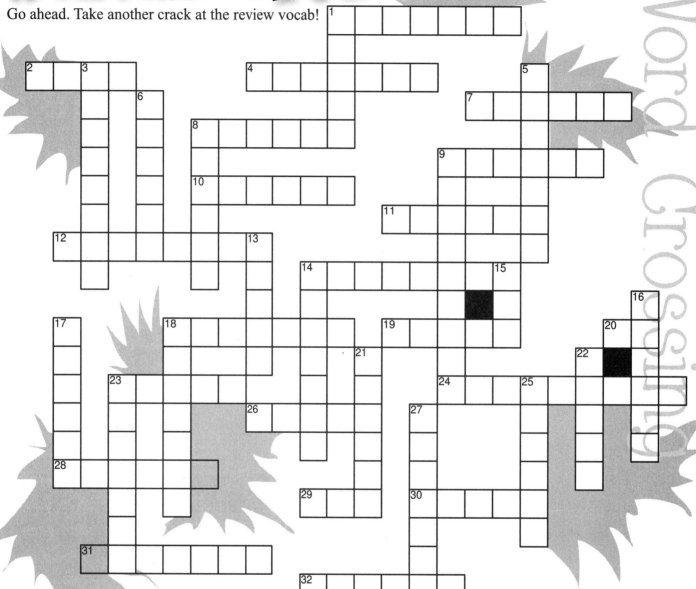

Across

1. flame
2. moon
4. tear
7. married
8. thanks
9. to announce
10. help, aid
11. tongue, language
12. battle
14. luxury, extravagance
18. help, aid
19. to help
20. it (nominative or accusative case)
23. call away
24. to marry
26. move
28. move
29. him (accusative case)
30. effort, services
31. deputy, lieutenant
32. shape, beauty

Down

1. shape, beauty
3. to announce
5. thanks
6. effort, services
8. sword
9. to announce
13. move
14. to praise
15. her (accusative case)
16. help, aid
17. war, battle
18. call away
21. move away
22. door
23. move away
25. door
27. memory

chapter 11

eō
is
it
īmus
ītis
eunt

ībam
ībās
ībat
ībāmus
ībātis
ībant

We need someone to
work the ballpark hot
dog stand today. Are
you ready to go?
Pardon the pun.

HOT DOG STAND

ībō
ībis
ībit
ībimus
ībitis
ībunt

Draw a line from each condiment bottle
part then circle the correct Latin parts
on each wiener. Use colored pencils.

SINGULAR · PLURAL
KETCHUP

1st Person
2nd Person
3rd Person
Spicy Mustard

PRESENT · IMPERFECT · FUTURE
RELISH

31

Plug 'n Play

We need a talented Latin student to try to connect all these Accusative Case Prepositions. Can you wire things correctly?

ad	super
extrā	inter
intrā	into
after	circā
secundum	ante
against	iuxtā
near	over, above, beyond
propter	across
before	between
over, above, on top of	per
along	outside
ultrā	among
apud	by, at, near
through	below
post	near
suprā	within
contrā	praeter
to, toward	in + acc.
around	ob
in front of	infrā
prope	beyond
sub + acc.	past
on account of	trāns
up to	

We had a bit of an accident. Fortunately, no one was hurt... except for the front fender. Can you unscramble the Latin words that were in the back seat? CLUE: these words are all from this week's vocabulary.

Fender Bender

AD, TO, AROWDT

☐☐ , ☐☐☐ , ☐☐☐☐☐☐
⟨6⟩

UAPD, NAMOG, YB, TA, ERAN

☐☐☐☐☐ , ☐☐☐☐☐☐ , ☐☐ , ☐☐ , ☐☐☐☐
⟨13⟩　　　　　　⟨8⟩

ĀCCRI, ONARDU

☐☐☐☐☐ , ☐☐☐☐☐☐
⟨4⟩

TONRĀC, AIGNATS

☐☐☐☐☐☐ , ☐☐☐☐☐☐☐
⟨5⟩

NI + CAC., IONT

☐☐ + ☐☐☐☐ . , ☐☐☐☐
⟨2⟩

RĀNFI, BWOEL

☐☐☐☐☐☐☐ , ☐☐☐☐☐
⟨10⟩

ĀRNIT, IITHNW

☐☐☐☐☐☐ , ☐☐☐☐☐☐

BO, NI FNTOR OF

☐☐ , ☐☐ ☐☐☐☐☐ ☐☐
⟨14⟩

PRE, OTHHRUG

☐☐☐☐ , ☐☐☐☐☐☐☐
⟨11⟩

ATEPRER, TAPS

☐☐☐☐☐☐☐ , ☐☐☐☐
⟨7⟩

PPREORT, NO AONCUTC OF

☐☐☐☐☐☐☐ , ☐☐ ☐☐☐☐☐☐ ☐☐
⟨9⟩　　⟨12⟩

BSU + CAC., UP TO

☐☐☐☐ + ☐☐☐☐ . , ☐☐ ☐☐
⟨15⟩　　⟨3⟩

ĀRTLU, ENYOBD

☐☐☐☐☐☐☐ , ☐☐☐☐☐☐
⟨1⟩

MESSAGE: ☐☐☐ ☐☐☐ ☐ ☐☐☐☐☐ – ☐☐ ¡☐☐☐!
　　　　　1 2 3　4 5 6　7　8 9 10 11　12 13　14 15

33

chapter 12

to carry

We've been hard at work cutting some wood out in the Lowe's backyard. Can you help their 4 boys carry the wood? Circle the correct parts of this irregular verb (meaning "to carry").

fertis	1st	2nd	3rd	Sing.	Plur.	Pres.	Imp.
ferēbam	1st	2nd	3rd	Sing.	Plur.	Pres.	Imp.
ferimus	1st	2nd	3rd	Sing.	Plur.	Pres.	Imp.
ferēbant	1st	2nd	3rd	Sing.	Plur.	Pres.	Imp.
ferēbāmus	1st	2nd	3rd	Sing.	Plur.	Pres.	Imp.
fers	1st	2nd	3rd	Sing.	Plur.	Pres.	Imp.
ferunt	1st	2nd	3rd	Sing.	Plur.	Pres.	Imp.
fert	1st	2nd	3rd	Sing.	Plur.	Pres.	Imp.
ferō	1st	2nd	3rd	Sing.	Plur.	Pres.	Imp.
ferēbās	1st	2nd	3rd	Sing.	Plur.	Pres.	Imp.
ferēbātis	1st	2nd	3rd	Sing.	Plur.	Pres.	Imp.
ferēbat	1st	2nd	3rd	Sing.	Plur.	Pres.	Imp.

Did you know?

Ticket!

Obesa cantavit
The fat lady has sung

SUGAR SNAP!

Can you bring order to this garden chaos? Figure out as much of the code box as you begin to reveal the hidden vocabulary words below. With a little bit of work, it should produce a harvest... and be a snap!

A	B	C	D	E	F	G	H	I	J	K	L	M	N	O	P	Q	R	S	T	U	V	W	X	Y	Z
				17				11									16			23	10				4

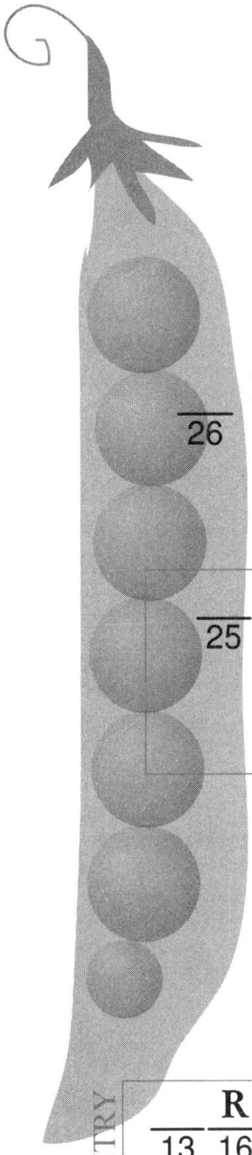
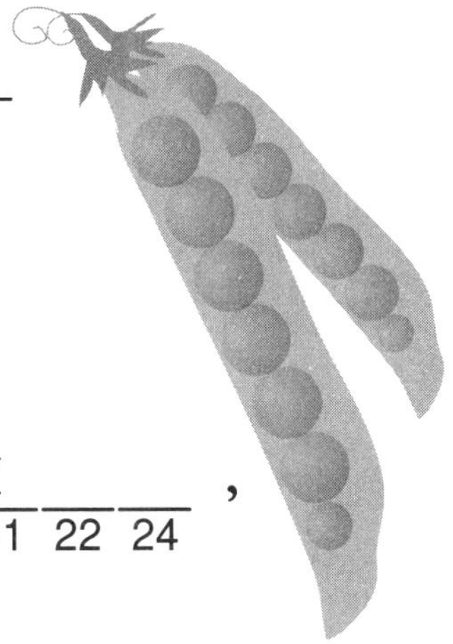

Ē _R E_, _U_ __
18 16 17 7, 18 23 25 18 3

_U_, _I__
14 23 8, 15 11 25 1

_U_, U__ER
20 23 12, 23 22 26 17 16

_ Ē, _R__, ____ERI__,
26, 3 16 18 8, 14 18 22 14 17 16 22 11 22 24

___U_
5 12 18 23 25

_EU_, __ __E E__E__ __ (ONE ENTRY)
25 17 22 23 20, 25 18 25 1 17 17 7 25 17 22 25 18 3

I_, I_, __
11 22, 11 22, 18 22

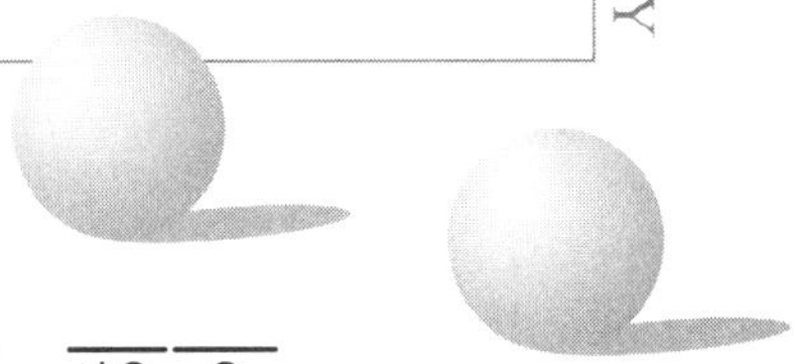

_R_E, I_ _R___ __
13 16 5 17, 11 22 3 16 18 22 25 18 3

Ā _R __, _R__, __
18 16 5 12, 3 16 18 8, 12 19

_RŌ, _E__RE, __ _E____ __ (ONE ENTRY)
13 16, 12 17 3 18 16 17, 18 22 12 17 1 5 21 3 18 3

_I_E, _I___U_
20 11 22 17, 15 11 25 1 18 23 25

_ŌR__, ___E-__-___E _I__
14 16 5 8, 3 5 14 17 - 25 18 - 3 5 14 17 15 11 25 1

THE OL' RUN AROUND

You know what you're doing here, don't you? Well, have it young lass/lad!

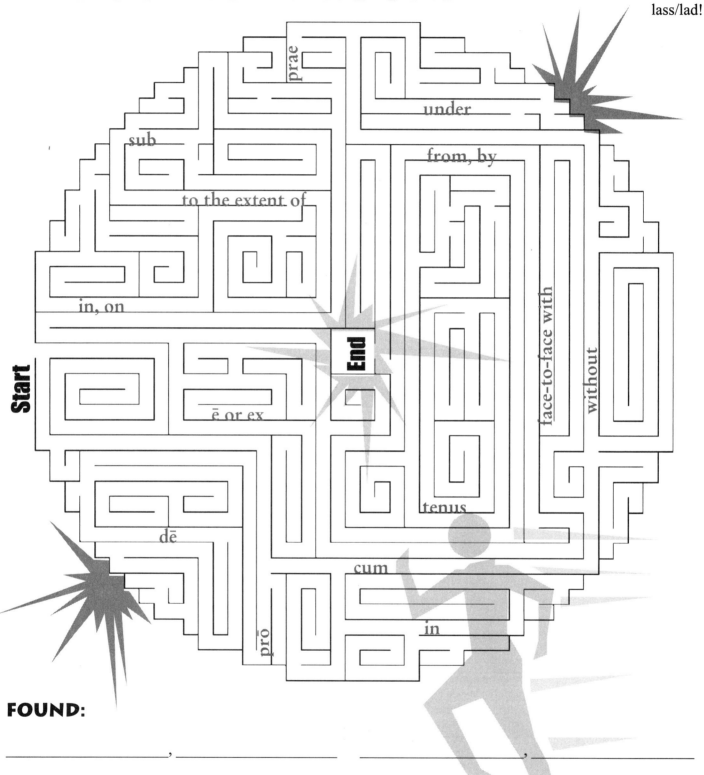

prae

under

sub

from, by

to the extent of

in, on

Start

face-to-face with

without

End

ē or ex

tenus

dē

cum

prō

in

FOUND:

_____, _____ _____,

_____, _____,

chapter
REVIEW 15

Wanna dig around and find the pockets of
English translations to the words below?
Check off the boxes on the Latin
translations that you find.

Gusher!

```
A Y C E I O A W N E U E L F W J B E F O R E Q Z V D T W I O
O M O B N V T R I B S D I R F M I K F Z R E T D D J W I N U
U W O T T E I H O T X J T O Y M S U V A Q L U L Q A P T F T
N N B N O R A V R U H J M M F A C E T O F A C E W I T H R S
E U D E G A B G V O N A C C O U N T O F A V O U T O F O O I
A Z V E F B N E A R U D L O B E T W E E N U P T O N I U N D
R T Y H R O Y E Y I W G W N A E B Y W P S V P C T O E T T E
D Y C K C V R A P O N R H C L D R O R U A C L C H X B Z O I
I U V O E F E T Q N S H E O Q B E L O W S D O E H N W F D
K N S Z D B R S O N X D T R N A K C U V A J T T E Y Y D B K
O P F D V E O A O N E U C N G Q K U Q M O N D D X G O X N M
H U U R C Y M J F B B A B I L E J B W Y G D T T T L R U Z C
W J I V O O B K D T D E R N J H E H P U B K W A E M G N C U
I D Q N E N Y D M W E V H G O V E R A B O V E O N T O P O F
T D O M P D T K N M E R X A R A S H Y F J T H F T H K I D U
H M Q X P F M O Q V J N E B L A C R O S S Q Y X O T U Z S D
I Q I Q I T K R F N J L E O G F R F F H J A F M F P G E V D
N Y N J N K K I B N B X E U G T O T O W A R D W N J R B B W
V R O B Q I U Z F W S C M T H B O F B J V L E U J Q F E Z L
X V N J W H B P Q T M G D C A V Z I M H E E D D L F T J V D
```

○ ad
○ ante
○ apud
○ circā
○ contrā
○ extrā
○ in + acc.
○ infrā
○ inter

○ intrā
○ iuxtā
○ ob
○ per
○ post
○ praeter
○ prope
⊗ propter
○ secundum

○ sub + acc.
○ super
○ suprā
○ trāns
○ ultrā
○ ā or ab
○ cōram
○ cum
○ dē

○ ē or ex
○ in
○ prae
○ prō
○ sine
○ sub
○ tenus

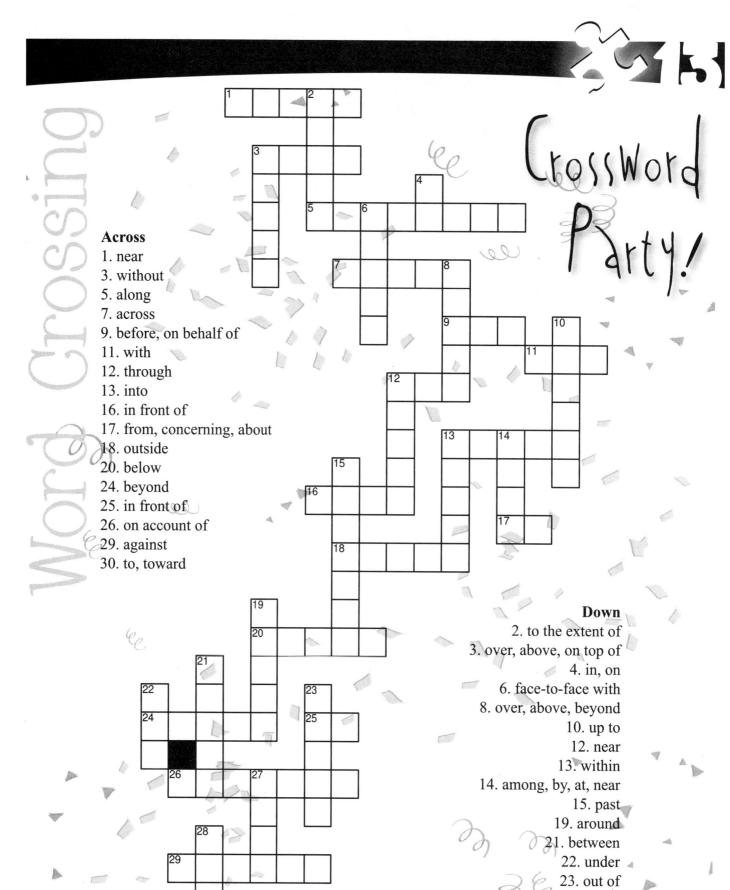

Crossword Party!

Word Crossing

Across

1. near
3. without
5. along
7. across
9. before, on behalf of
11. with
12. through
13. into
16. in front of
17. from, concerning, about
18. outside
20. below
24. beyond
25. in front of
26. on account of
29. against
30. to, toward

Down

2. to the extent of
3. over, above, on top of
4. in, on
6. face-to-face with
8. over, above, beyond
10. up to
12. near
13. within
14. among, by, at, near
15. past
19. around
21. between
22. under
23. out of
27. after
28. from, by

Budding review...

ORSSMEPUT, LTAS

☐☐☐☐☐☐☐☐☐☐ , ☐☐☐☐
　　16　　　　　　　　　　22　7

ACETR, CETRIAN

☐☐☐☐☐ , ☐☐☐☐☐☐☐
　　10

NUMRĪE, MRBENU, ERMSEAU

☐☐☐☐☐☐ , ☐☐☐☐☐☐ , ☐☐☐☐☐☐
　　　　　　　　19　9

MVIUN, IENW

☐☐☐☐☐ , ☐☐☐☐
3　　　　　　　15　13

ŌRHAE, RUHO

☐☐☐☐☐ , ☐☐☐☐
23　18　2

EERAMMO, OYMREM

☐☐☐☐☐☐☐ , ☐☐☐☐☐☐
5　　　　　　　　　　　　24

MŌTAIR, TO AYMRR

☐☐☐☐☐☐ , ☐☐ ☐☐☐☐☐
　　　　　　　　　　　　1

AĪVUDI, ELHP, DAI

☐☐☐☐☐☐ , ☐☐☐☐ , ☐☐☐
　　12　　　　8　14　21　　　4

USUNCMDE, AGOLN

☐☐☐☐☐☐☐☐ , ☐☐☐☐☐
11　17

ISNE, HOTUTIW

☐☐☐☐ , ☐☐☐☐☐☐☐
　　　6　　　　20

Hints

without
along
help, aid
to marry
memory
hour
wine
number, measure
certain
last

Secret Phrase

☐☐☐☐☐☐ ☐☐☐ ☐☐☐☐☐☐
1　2　3　4　5　6　　7　8　9　　10　11　12　13　14　15

☐☐☐☐☐☐☐☐☐ !
12　16　17　18　19　20　21　22　23　24

chapter H

perfume!

All these fancy perfumes are named with numbers these days. Will you help label the price tags in Latin? The store's management thanks you!

Math Blitz!

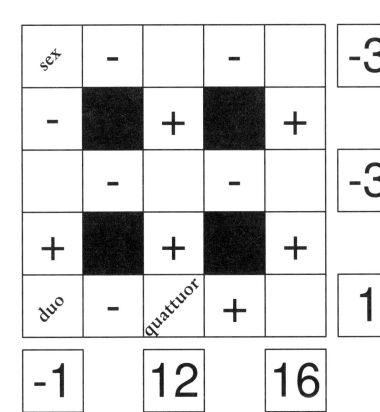

Like math? For this puzzle you'll have to use the Latin numbers for 1 through 9 to fill the spaces in the grid and complete each numerical expression.

NOTE: Each number is used only once. You must use addition/subtraction to complete this puzzle.

First grid:

quattuor	+		septem	+		13
+	■	+	■	+	
	+		+		15
+	■	+	■	+	
trēs	+		+	quinque	17

Column totals: 8   24   13

NOTE: Each number is used only once. You must use addition & subtraction to complete this puzzle.

Second grid:

sex	-		-		-3
-	■	+	■	+	
	-		-		-3
+	■	+	■	+	
duo	-	quattuor	+		1

Column totals: -1   12   16

LFC

SUGAR SMACKOLAS!

We found this tough little game on the back of a cereal box. Make sure not to get too wired on all that sugar!

NUTRITIONAL GUIDE
Calories 160
Serving size: 3 oz.
Vitamin A - 45%
Vitamin C - 50%
Vitamin B+ - 01%

This food product may be found hazardous if eaten after 10:00 pm at night. Please consult a doctor if you plan to operate heavy equiment or go snow sledding.

Coupon
Merely buy 154 boxes of this cereal and receive $1.50 off your next purchase

0935 355 3232 123

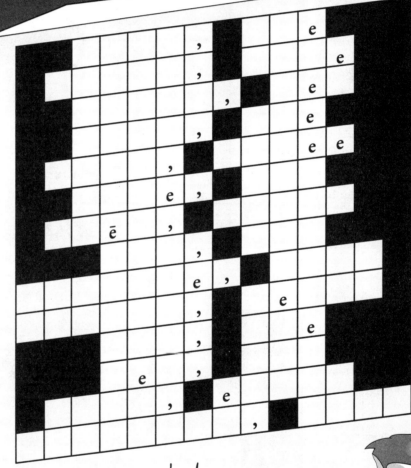

Eeeeeek!

Captain Sugar-Cube says, "Help us figure out the puzzle above and we'll include a prize in the box!" Most of this week's vocabulary is here. Figure out what goes where and finish the grid!

This was all that we found in the box other than sugar-laden cereal. That's the prize??

chapter 15

ORDINAL Numbers

13. tenth
16. seventh
17. third
19. sixth
20. eighth
21. sixth
23. ninth
24. second
25. sixth
26. tenth

Across
1. fifth
4. first
9. first
10. ninth
11. fifth

Down
1. fourth
2. seventh
3. third
5. second
6. fourth
7. tenth
8. seventh
11. fourth
12. eighth

14. fifth
15. ninth
18. third
20. eighth
22. second

Puzzle Path

It's no yellow brick road, but if you follow it & fill in the declension of **ūnus** as you go, you'll be a better Latin student!

Masculine
Ablative

Neuter
Ablative

Neuter
Genitive

Feminine
Accusative

Masculine
Genitive

Masculine
Nominative

Masculine
Accusative

Neuter
Dative

Feminine
Genitive

Feminine
Nominative

Feminine
Dative

Did you know?

Ticket!

Pactum serva
Keep the faith

Neuter
Accusative

Masculine
Dative

Neuter
Nominative

FINISHED!

Well done. Now click your heels and you'll be home.
What? You're homeschooled? Well... it worked!

Feminine
Ablative

Awards Banquet

Yes, your team placed!
Congratulations.
Can you help all the judges
figure out which award
is which? Write the Latin
translation on
each award.

9TH

3RD

10TH

4TH

5TH

8TH

1ST

2ND

6TH

7TH

Did you know?
Ticket!
Canis meus
id comedit
My dog ate it

chapter 16

Dunkin' D's

There's a new artsy coffee shop in town. They want you to dip your biscotti in the correct blends of coffee. You don't like coffee?! Well, can you dunk 'em correctly anyway?

duo • nominative

duārum • genitive

duo • accusative

duōbus • ablative

duae • nominative

duās • accusative

duābus • ablative

duōrum • genitive

duābus • dative

FEMININE

MASCULINE

NEUTER

AUTUMN

Time to rake the leaves. And while you're at it, here's a crisp little cross word to go along with your mug of hot cocoa (for you who don't like coffee) for when you're done.

Word Crossing

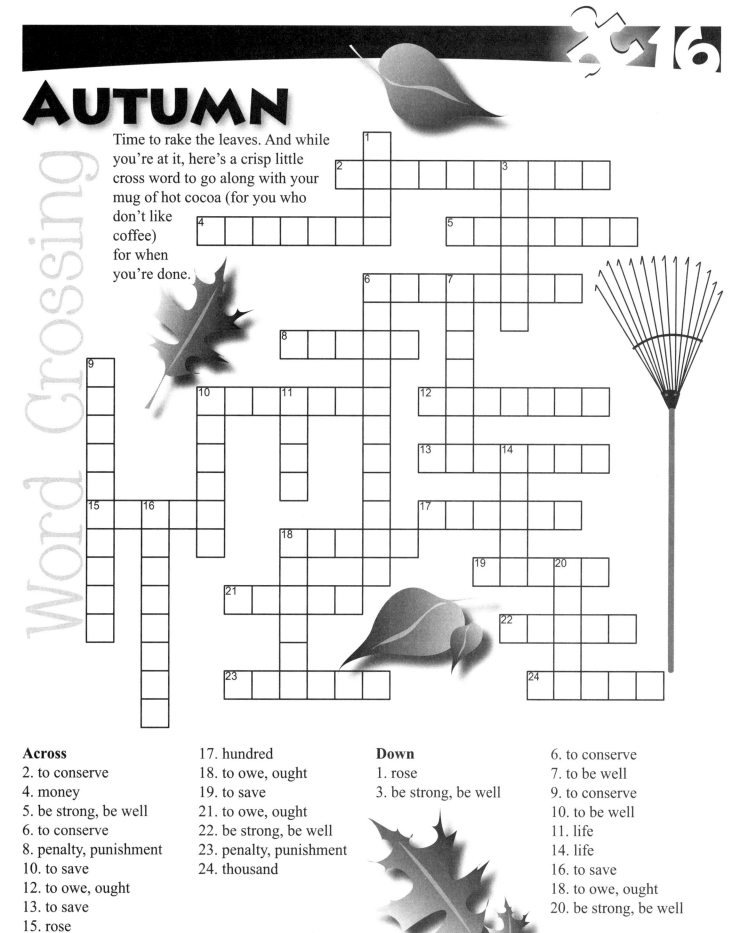

Across
2. to conserve
4. money
5. be strong, be well
6. to conserve
8. penalty, punishment
10. to save
12. to owe, ought
13. to save
15. rose
17. hundred
18. to owe, ought
19. to save
21. to owe, ought
22. be strong, be well
23. penalty, punishment
24. thousand

Down
1. rose
3. be strong, be well
6. to conserve
7. to be well
9. to conserve
10. to be well
11. life
14. life
16. to save
18. to owe, ought
20. be strong, be well

Happy Birthday!

Can you figure out what in what year these famous people had their birthdays?
Use your Latin noodle to translate them (from Roman into Arabic or Arabic into Roman).

FAMOUS PERSON	BIRTHDAY!
Joan of Arc - MCDXII A.D.	
Sir Francis Bacon - MDLXI A.D.	
Blaise Pascal - 1623 A.D.	
George Fredrick Handel - 1685 A.D.	
Wolfgang Amadeus Mozart - MDCCLVII	
Davy Crockett - 1786	
Abraham Lincoln - MDCCCIX	
Robert Louis Stevenson - 1850	
Madame Curie - 1867	
Greta Garbo - 1905	

chapter 17

SLEEPER HIT!!

Hey, don't go to sleep on me! With this puzzle you first translate the words below into Latin then find 'em somewhere in the jumble to the left.

A K O H C U T N O Z R O	wisdom _____
M I M T U S O M N U S W	wisdom _____
H I J B L T E L A O Z R	care _____
S S H P P O O R Y M I A	care _____
G U W H A X O R B H F E	fault, blame, sin_____
S A P I E N T I A E C E	fault, blame, sin_____
S P H Z R L C A L T E H	river bank _____
Q A S O M N Ī A G M R W	river bank _____
Y S P I U R C U V X V I	sleep _____
K C I I F J O G S U U L	sleep _____
X Q R O E V O A K H S R	angle _____
I F U R W N O V X J C Ī	angle _____
A X Y L Z S T P Y I P P	pebble _____
I N U X C V F I V C B A	pebble _____
C T G J S A R K A A D E	hole _____
M U I U P K L N W L I I	hole _____
L D L R L E O C A C N L	stag, deer _____
R M Q P Z Ī G S U U A R	stag, deer _____
B Ī C S A A N G U L U S	
L M P V V L L D L U Ī G	
P F V A H X E O P S Q J	
I T I C A D B L C B Z R	
H U Z A F K U I N W M H	
Z S S V S K C K S Q B L	
Y H P Ī T J E E R P B S	
J P X W C Ū R A E H D P	
Y O W A C H V P O M C H	
D E G M X Z Ī N U V T T	
V C Ū R A A T K D M K N	
R G G X H O C H P K N H	

Zzzzzzzz!

3 Musketeers:
Inner office memo

Unfortunately, the 3 Musketeers lost a long-standing member to overseas outsourcing. Now they're looking to hire a replacement. Will you help D'Artagnan review these 5 resumes below by circling the correct attributes that each candidate should have (to match up with the declension of **trēs**?)

Name: Sir Genitive
Skillset: trēs
neuter
tribus
Quickbooks
Masculine
trium
Feminine
Win XP
tria
Microsoft Office
Photocopier
Stapler

NAME: COUNT NOMINATIVE
EXPERIENCE:
TRIA – NEUTER
TRIBUS – MASC./FEM.
I KNOW HOW TO USE
CONFERENCE CALL
ANSWERING MACHINE
TRĒS
MASC./FEM.
PENCIL SHARPENER

Name: Madame Dative
Qualifications:
Copymachine collate
tres – masc. tribus – fem.
tribus – neuter. coffee mach.,
group leader. tribus – masc.,
tria – neuter. typewriter,
newsletter layout.

Name: Duchess Accusative
Background:
tribus, trium, staple remover
letter opener, tribu-a-bebu
tres, mas., UPS shipping, fem.,
neuter, tria, trio,
Some Photoshop work
Instant messaging

Name: Mr. Ablative
Good at: Water cooler (new bottle install)
tria - neuter, tribus - masc., trium - fem.
tribus - fem., network marketing,
bartering (mostly with chickens)

Firecracker Latin!

Across
1	c	o	n	t	r	ā

Yes, the answers are given to you... but it's all about the questions!

In order to be an effective Latin whipper-snapper, can you fill in all the lines below to make a BANG?

KA-BLAM!

Across

3. _____
5. _____
7. _____
9. _____
13. _____
14. _____
15. _____
18. _____
19. _____
21. _____

22. _____
24. _____
25. _____

Down

1. _____
2. _____
4. _____
6. _____
8. _____
10. _____

11. _____
12. _____
13. _____
14. _____
16. _____
17. _____
20. _____
21. _____
23. _____

chapter
REVIEW 18

A Numbers Game

Wowzers! Inside this box of letters are **90 Latin words** (some review words as well) for numbers. Just how many can you find?

More importantly, how many can you translate when you find them?

```
S S S Z C P D C S E M P Q D Q S H X M Q Y W B S N
S A L O Ū R Ē U E E Z D E U D E S H M U D I L A V
P A P R R I B L R L C I Ē C I X E M F I N O V E M
J O L I A M U P V A A U X B Ū N P N Ō N U S T T K
T G E V E A Ī A Ā I S E N T E N T I A T V A L E Ō
C E K N E N T E R T I U S D V Ō I U J U C A V U S
O P R E A Ō T Q E D D W A E U A M A S M T R I A E
N O Z T A E F I Q Ē Ē S Q N X M U S O M N U S P O
S E P T I M U M A B B O U C G T S C A L C U L U S
E N X R D U D T J Ī Ē M A E V U U R R Ī P A L J T
R A E Ē D Q M U Z T R N T R C Y L S D U O W W Q H
V M P S A U D Q O U E Ī T V T X Q Ī Q U A R T U M
Ā Ī W C S A A U Y M U E U U Q S S Y S C U L P A V
V L T S C R Q U I N T A O S Y R O Ū E V A L Ē R E
Ī L X A Q T J O R P W W R U O D C N R T F F T T K
Z E D N T U F X C S E R V Ā V Ī T U V R O S A A C
J J H Z G S M Q C T O V P L I V A S Ā A K F S H Ŭ
D H O P S E P T I M A C Ī C N F V U T N P D E I R
T Q R O S A E N H F N V T T O C U A U G R S X W A
D A U Ī M C K C J P Z B U A A N M R M U I E T K R
S E N I P U O J W W Y B O S V E S S W L M C U I A
V A C Ō N A S N C A L C U L Ī A T E A U U U A B Q
S A L E N Q E D S E X T U M I R I K R S S N K V F
C E L V M U U I E E Q S E C U N D U S V E D N Ū Ī
O E P U Ē Y M E N C R V A L Ī T U M T D Ō A Ō N C
C C R T Ī R T R L U I V S E R V Ō K N E P P N A O
R S T V E C E N T U M M Ā P R I M U M C R D A Q J
T C A Ō Ī M Z T S M V T U R N C I R Q I E T U X P
A T F C O N S E R V Ā T U M E Ū N U M M A G I A X
K N P R D R J D E C I M U S X F G L R A B K E A E
```

NUMBER CRUNCHING

Below are some simple math problems. They shouldn't involve complicated math problems, except that they all involve roman numbers. Put on your little thinking beanie and get crackin'!

PROBLEM 1

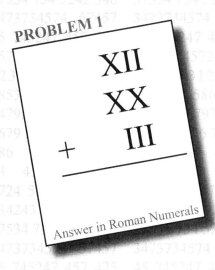

XII
XX
+ III
———
Answer in Roman Numerals

PROBLEM 2

LIV
CCCIII
+ IX
———
Answer in Roman Numerals

PROBLEM 3

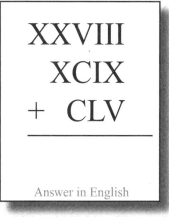

XXVIII
XCIX
+ CLV
———
Answer in English

PROBLEM 4

XVI
IX
+MDXI
———
Answer in English

PROBLEM 5

MMCMCDLXXIII
MMMCCCXXXIII
MDCCCLXX
+
———————
Answer in English

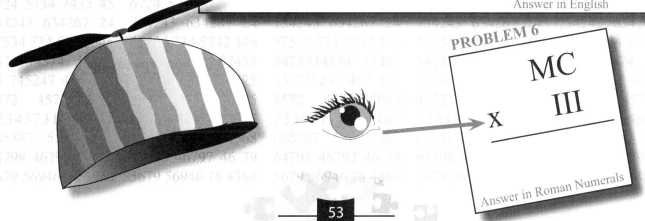

PROBLEM 6

MC
III
X
———
Answer in Roman Numerals

DERIVATIVE SQUARE DANCE

There's a big country dance tonight and you're invited. Only thing is that we need someone to help the Latin on one side of the hall to team up correctly with the English derivatives on the other side. Wanna help?

trēs, tria	conservation, conserve, conservative
somnus, -ae	serve, servant, servile, serf
ūnus, ūna, ūnum	September (originally it was the 7th month), septet, septuplets
decimus, -a, -um	quarter, quartet, quart, quadruplets
decem	six, sextet, sextuplets
dēbeō	second, secondary
calculus, -ae	care, cure, curator
cavus, -ī	glory, glorification, glorify
quartus, -a, -um	somnolent, insomnia, somnambulist (sleep-walker)
angulus, -ae	angle, angular
sex	quart, quarter
septem	valor, valiant, prevail
centum	one, unit, unity, union, united, unite
mille	decimate
conservō	century, centimeter, centipede, cent, centennial
servō	millennium, millennial, million
valeō	December (originally the 10th month), decade, decimate
rosa, -ae	prime, primary, primal, primeval
primus, -a, -um	debt, debit, indebted, indebt
secundus, -a, -um	three, triple, triplets, trio, tricycle, triad, trinity, triangle
cūra, -ae	rose, rosy
quattuor	calculate, calculator, Calculus
glōria, -ae	cave, cavern, cavernous
silentium, -ī	silent

chapter 19

Genitive Plural

-ēs

Accusative Plural

Nominative Singular

-ī

Dative Singular

-ibus

Ablative Singular

-is

-em

-e

Nominative Plural

Genitive Singular

Accusative Singular

CLAMMY

-x

-um

Ablative Plural

Dative Plural

Match up the pearls with the correct Latin clams. Yeah, I know... Who's ever heard of a Latin clam? Work with me will ya?!

-ēs

-ibus

WEEDS

Across
1. to respond
1. to sit
1. to do the broad stroke
5. to terrify, frighten
6. king
6. to respond
6. to laugh, giggle or sputter (out the nose)
8. to terrify, frighten
10. (f) citizenship, state, commonwealth
13. to sit
13. to stand
15. (f) sister
16. to sit
17. to sit
17. sister
19. (m)king
20. citizenship, state, commonwealth
22. king
22. to respond
23. to laugh, smile
24. to respond

Down
1. to laugh, smile
1. to get a thorn in the finger
2. to terrify, frighten
3. leader, first one, prince
4. (c) leader, first one, prince
5. to fear, be afraid of
5. to sit
6. to laugh, smile
7. king
9. to laugh, smile
11. sister
11. to sleep
11. to fear, be afraid of
12. youth, young person
14. to fear, be afraid of
14. to jump, as for joy
15. to sit
15. to pickle, or to eat the afore mentioned
18. to king, as in checkers
18. sister
18. to sit
21. to terrify, frighten
21. to get spooked by the dark or a creepy old saturday afternoon movie

Are you willing to help "weed" the garden below.? Find the correct questions to the cross word above & complete the puzzle.

ROUND ABOUT

Weave your way around the maze until you hit the pockets of Latin. Translate before moving on. Can you head the round about way and still finish?

_____, sister
_____, (c) leader, first one, prince
_____, (f) citizenship, state, commonwealth
_____, to respond
_____, to laugh, smile

_____, to sit

_____, to fear, be afraid of

_____, king

_____, to respond

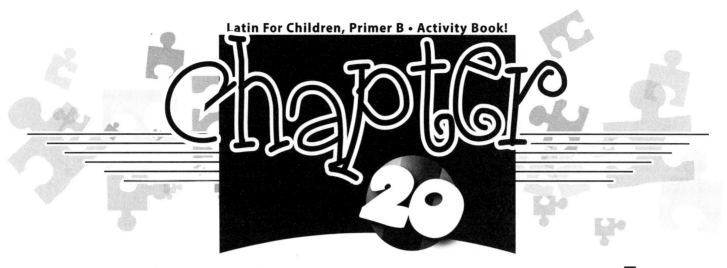

DOUBLE [2x] TROUBLE!

In here is this week's vocabulary (English translation) but it looks like you've got your work cut out for you. You'll find each word twice! Can you find them all and translate them into Latin when you find them?

```
A Z F M N W K M W B Y F S V K P O B Y Z Q J M O S
R I N S K P K K A Q R E B O E A X L Y O I F Y C H
W S H I P D C Q L M S O O D U R R R D E W E O I I
F A T U V J G X L T O X T X E E O B A M D U U T P
T D L P M S O Y E V Z T J H V N K X T P A Q N I M
V R S L X F R K D H C B H F E T G J F M O N G Z O
G K I J E R X S T U P X U E V R W D B I V B P E T
Q C W B D D W K O F A T H E R C I T I Z E N E N H
C K I Y E N T C W B R O T H E R T R I B E L R M E
Q L Z N J T F O N N M L Z O H Y N I W L N J S D R
S Q A I P N W A W C G D H U S H M E U R X T O X E
C L A N G I I J T N E M E G N C C H N U S O N I Q
K B P W Z T K W X H P A R E N T I R T O T J F D U
J Z N P I L Q A X M E N O K I K T T B C B E I A M
Y O U N G P E R S O N R L Z T H Y J Y M Q R I M I
```

_____, _____   _____, _____   _____, _____

_____, _____   _____, _____   _____, _____

_____, _____   _____, _____   _____, _____

_____, _____   _____, _____   _____, _____

_____, _____   _____, _____   _____, _____

_____, _____   _____, _____   _____, _____

WORD(S) FOUND/TRANSLATED

Smuggler

A box of Latin words was found by the Customs Department. Can you help shuffle these words and find the Latin word that is scrambled in each garbled mess? Do this correctly and you'll find the hidden catch phrase!

HINT: Hints can be found, if you need 'em, on the top of the next page.

1. RTĀRFE
2. ĀRTISFR
3. ETMĀR
4. ITMĀSR
5. REĀPT
6. TRĀSPI
7. ĪISCV
8. VSCIĪ
9. NRSĒPA
10. RATINPES
11. ĀNVIS
12. ĀINSV
13. IUEIVNS
14. EVIISNU
15. SNXEE
16. SISEN
17. RBUS
18. SURBI
19. ĒNSG
20. ENSTIG

Catch Phrase

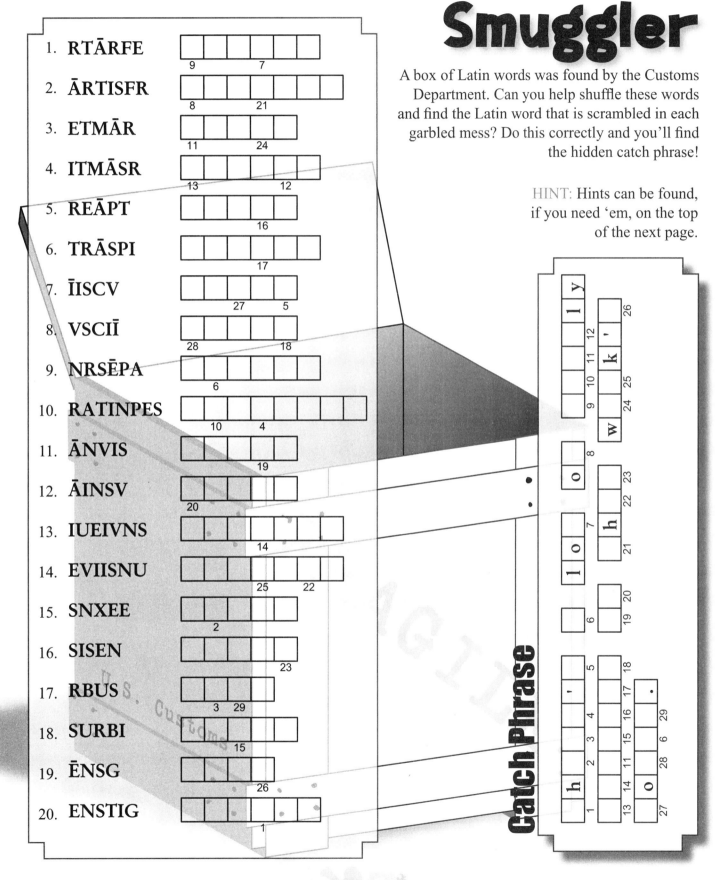

59

HINTS!

1. (m) brother
2. (m) brother
3. (f) mother
4. (f) mother
5. (m) father
6. (m) father
7. (c, i) citizen
8. (c, i) citizen
9. (c, i) parent
10. (c, i) parent
11. (f, i) ship
12. (f, i) ship
13. (c, i) young person (age 20-40)
14. (c, i) young person (age 20-40)
15. (m) old man
16. (m) old man
17. (f, i) walled town, city
18. (f, i) walled town, city
19. (f, i) clan, tribe
20. (f, i) clan, tribe

Star catching

Come on!! Surely you've heard of that old popular song titled, *"Fishing on a star?"* Wait a minute... that's not right. Oh well,... these 3rd declension (i-stem) nouns could use some help. You'll need to draw a hook into all those stars that offer correct Latin. Can you pull in your catch without pulling in an old boot?

Did you know?

Ticket!

Credidi me felem vidisse!

I thought I saw a puddy tat!

HOME

Across
3. (m) brother
4. (f) sister
7. to sit
8. to terrify, frighten
10. to terrify, frighten
12. to laugh, smile
14. (f,i) walled town, city
16. (c) leader, first one, prince
17. citizenship, state, commonwealth
18. to laugh, smile
19. to sit
21. (c, i) citizen
22. (f) mother
25. (m) father
27. (f, i) clan, tribe
30. to terrify, frighten
31. (f, i) clan, tribe
32. (f,i) walled town, city
33. to laugh, smile

Down
1. (f, i) ship
2. (c, i) parent
4. sister
5. (m) old man
6. youth, young person
9. to respond
11. to respond
13. to fear, be afraid of
15. (c, i) youth, young person
16. (c, i) parent
17. (c, i) citizen
20. (f) mother
23. king
24. to fear, be afraid of
26. (m) father
28. to terrify, frighten
29. to sit

VISITORS

KEEPING SECRETS

Can you keep a secret? We can't! At the bottom of this puzzle we've given away the secret phrase. Can you unscramble some of this week's vocabulary words and use the Latin phrase below as a help if you need it?

RTERFA, BEHRROT
[ ][ ][ ][ ][ ][ ], [ ][ ][ ][ ][ ][ ][ ]
6   12 8

EGSN, CNAL
[ ][ ][ ][ ], [ ][ ][ ]
3   19

MAETR, ETOHRM
[ ][ ][ ][ ][ ], [ ][ ][ ][ ][ ]
14   2

SXNEE, LOD MNA
[ ][ ][ ][ ][ ], [ ][ ][ ] [ ][ ][ ]
4   21 22

RTEAP, FTRHAE
[ ][ ][ ][ ][ ], [ ][ ][ ][ ][ ][ ]
10

SEIIUNV, UONYG NOSRPE
[ ][ ][ ][ ][ ][ ][ ], [ ][ ][ ][ ][ ] [ ][ ][ ][ ][ ][ ]
5

CSIVI, EIINCTZ
[ ][ ][ ][ ][ ], [ ][ ][ ][ ][ ][ ]
20   11 1

VASIN, SHPI
[ ][ ][ ][ ][ ], [ ][ ][ ][ ]
16 18

PESARN, ENATPR
[ ][ ][ ][ ][ ][ ], [ ][ ][ ][ ][ ][ ]
23 7   13

AIPTELUS, RTEETL
[ ][ ][ ][ ][ ][ ][ ][ ], [ ][ ][ ][ ][ ][ ]
9   15   17

[T][H][E] "[N][O][T] [S][O] [S][E][C][R][E][T]"
1 2 3   4 5 6   7 8   9 10 11 12 13 14

[L][A][T][I][N] [C][O][D][E].
15 16 17 18 19 20 21 22 23

62

The submarine wolf-pack has been destroying our transport ships. Can you captain the battleship, connect the correct parts of **nāvis,** and eliminate the threat?

Battleship

21

USS LATIN

ABL.

NOM.

DAT.

ACC.

GEN.

nāves

nāvī

navibus

nave

nāvis

navem

navēs

navium

chapter 22

A LITTLE DUCT TAPE, PLEASE

	NOMINATIVE		DATIVE	ACCUSATIVE	
♂				hunc (this)	
♀		haec			
					hōc

Table header: SINGULAR

Things have been falling apart around here. We're in need of a good handywoman or handyman to fix this chart back to what it should be. Want the part time job?

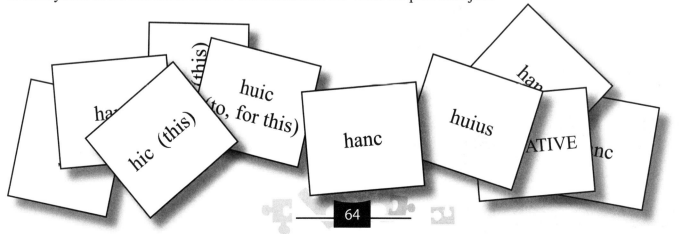

hic (this) · huic (to, for this) · hanc · huius · hic (this) · ATIVE · nc · ha...

Down Home Cooking

Can you help Mamma whip up a wholesome & tasty treat by finishing this puzzle?

Home Cookin'

Across
2. to deny
5. to deny
6. (f) art, skill
11. to strengthen, assert, affirm
13. to declare
15. (m) pain, anguish, sorrow
17. to build, erect establish
19. (m) love
20. (m) fear
22. to deny
24. (m) fear
25. to visit frequently
26. to fill, to celebrate

Down
1. to fill, to celebrate
3. to visit frequently
4. to strengthen, assert, affirm
6. (f) art, skill
7. to build, erect establish
8. (f) will
9. to declare
10. to build, erect establish
12. (f) will
14. to build, erect establish
15. to declare
16. to declare
18. to strengthen, assert, affirm

21. (m) love
22. to deny
23. (m) pain, anguish, sorrow

Chain-Gang

The prison gang is out on the railroads again laying track in the hot sun. Can you help out the crew (plural demonstrative pronoun hic, haec, hoc) to help alleviate some of the weight of these chains? The first one is done for you.

Masculine — Nominative
hī (these)
Neuter — Genitive
Neuter — Accusative
Feminine — Dative
Masculine — Ablative

Neuter — Dative

Masculine — Accusative
Neuter — Ablative
Feminine — Nominative
Masculine — Dative
Feminine — Genitive

Feminine — Accusative
Masculine — Genitive
Neuter — Nominative
Feminine — Ablative

Okay, we've got a bit of funny business going on here. Somebody put in some wacky parts to this cross-word puzzle that don't even fit! That don't even have real answers!! Can you make your way through this puzzle and sort out the real questions from the nutty ones?

Across

2. (m) labor, work
5. (m, i) mountain
6. (m) the sun
7.5. (n) banana peeler
8. (m) tooth
10. (f) wife
11. (f) voice
12. (f) night
13. (m) the sun

14. (f,i) clothing, garment
15. (m) victor
201. italian sports car

Down

1. (f) night
2. (f) light
3. (m) tooth
3½. (p) holiday meal left-over
4. (m) victor

5. (m, i) mountain
7. (m) labor, work
9. (f) light
10. (f) wife
10¾. close to shear nonsense but not quite
11. (f,i) clothing, garment
14. (f) voice

Corn-ucopia

It's harvest time! Help us pick the corn by filling in the blanks with this puzzle using the demonstrative pronoun ille, illa, illud.

Plur. Dat. Fem.

Sing. Dat. Masc.

Plur. Dat. Neut.

Sing. Gen. Masc.

Plur. Acc. Neut.

Sing. Dat. Neut.

Plur. Abl. Fem.

Plur. Acc. Masc.

Sing. Gen. Fem.

Plur. Gen. Fem.

Sing. Abl. Fem.

Sing. Dat. Neut.

Sing. Dat. Fem.

Sing. Gen. Fem.

Plur. Abl. Neut.

Plur. Dat. Masc.

Sing. Acc. Masc.

Plur. Gen. Masc.

Sing. Gen. Neut.

Plur. Nom. Masc.

Sing. Abl. Masc.

Sing. Nom. Fem.

Sing. Acc. Neut.

Sing. Acc. Fem.

Plur. Acc. Fem.

Plur. Gen. Neut.

Plur. Abl. Masc.

Sing. Nom. Masc.

Sing. Abl. Neut.

Plur. Nom. Fem.

Hmmm...
Seems that there
is one corn cob
(box) missing.
Know which one?

iN A BiND to FiND

I see you're already looking but what are you finding? Can you find all of this week's vocab and one other word you've had in the past?

```
N M L W N V H E V H E Q G
Z R A U D L I Y E D R D J
A D B A I J M C S V I C E
F C Ō K U E B I T E Z Z S
U D R A K F N S I Ō Z N D
C O I N F F O Ō S D R M O
L X S G O H U L D Z H I B
C A K H E X T I E P S H S
V Ō C I S L Q S N R R X L
V D Q F G Ū C A T P Y T A
U I R W E C B Z I S O P V
R Z C T E I P H S U H T O
M O N T I S L R M D T I X
V G J Y O V B A P R Q X P
B N J F Q R R K B P C W L
A P K A C I M C E O K Q O
X W Q Y F A E J A U R B M
T N M M A M O R T U U M X
E I O T D O S Ō L H W W E
D M A C D E C B B W R N K
Y M G X T E U O O O T Z S
G N G G P I N X O H C M L
K D S M U K S S Ō U X O R
V E S T I S T E R R D N R
J N T T N W I H F G I S F
L U X Z P E O Q J N Q S I
A B W F Z K J J N W X H M
Z R W M B Q Q G W E F H Y
S X V R Q V X B X A S M D
Y J U T Z S N T U J Q A B
```

Extra word found & translated:

Maze Blaze

How fast can you make it through this maze? Just be careful of the croc. pit!!

Start

Finish

Latin found (translated):

1 _____

2 _____

3 _____

Labels in maze: labōris, uxor, noctis, labor, vox, sōlis, montis, victor, nox, lux, sōl, vōcis, nice dentis

chapter 2

COME, VOLŌ WITH US!

2. to keep, preserve

1. (f) law, contract

2. to keep, preserve

1. to sin, make a mistake

1. to fly

2. (m) ancestor, originator, supporter

1. to take an oath

2. to fly

2. to keep, to take an oath

2. to keep, preserve

1.

1. (m) judge

2. to take an oath

1. to take an oath

2. to take an oath

1. (m) judge

1. to condemn, punish

2. to fly

2. (f) power

2. to influence, authority

2. (f) power

2. to condemn, contract

1. (f) law, punish

These radio controlled airplanes are getting all mixed up. Which RC controller goes with which RC airplane?

1. iurāre
2. conservō

1. iūdicis
2. iurāre

2. damnāre
1. lex

1. iurāre
2. volātum

2. conservō
1. lēgis

1. volātum
2. auctor

1. peccō
2. conservō

2. potestās
1. iurātum

1. auctōritātis
2. potestās

1. damnō
2. volātum

2. iurō
1. iūdicis

POTSHOT!

We were aiming for the soda can... honest! Can you help us fix the Latin chants below for the demonstrative pronoun **iste, ista, istud**?

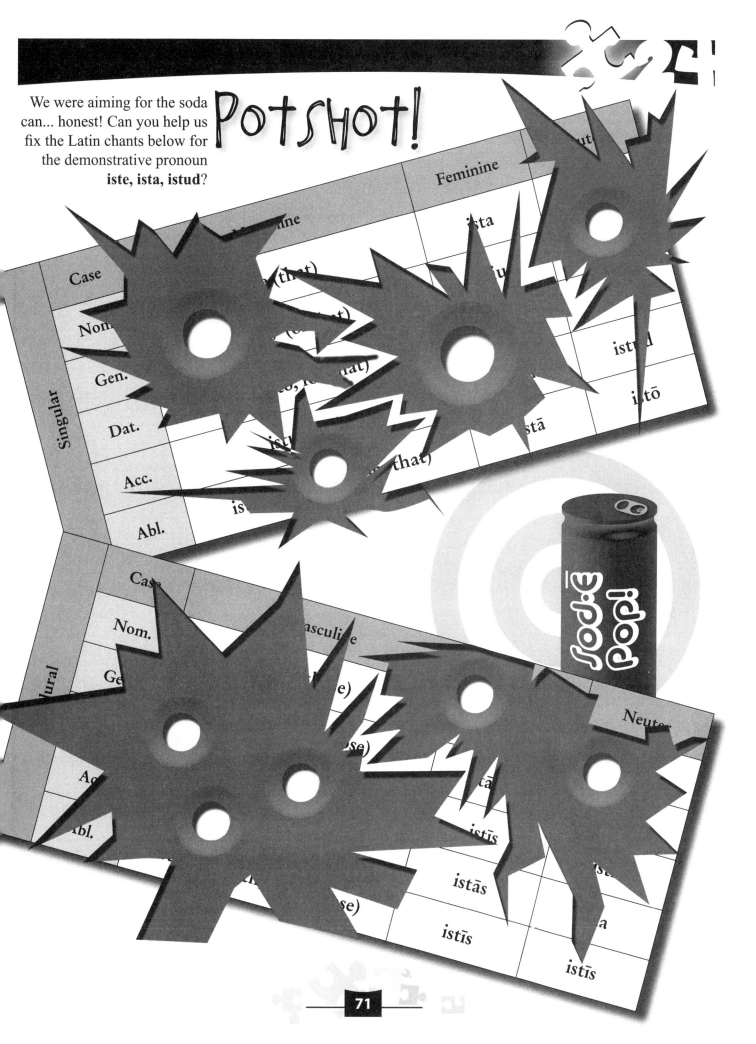

Case		Feminine	
		ista	
			istud
			istō
		istā	

Singular — Case, Nom., Gen., Dat., Acc., Abl.

(that) ... (o ... that) ... (eo, ... tud) ... (is ... that) ... is ...

Case			Neuter
Nom.	Masculine		
Ge		istā	
A		istīs	
bl.		istās	
		istīs	
		istīs	

Plural

SodaPopi

Cryptic Code Cruncher

Yup. these are words from this week's vocab. Can you crack 'em all? Take your time.

A	B	C	D	E	F	G	H	I	J	K	L	M	N	O	P	Q	R	S	T	U	V	W	X	Y	Z
		18							20								17	9	4	2	23				

$$\frac{V}{2}\frac{}{16}\frac{}{7}\quad \frac{\bar{O}}{}, \quad \frac{T}{9}\frac{}{16}\frac{}{26}\frac{}{7}\frac{}{24}$$

$$\frac{V}{2}\frac{}{16}\frac{}{7}\quad \frac{\bar{A}}{9}\frac{T}{4}\frac{U}{1}, \quad \frac{T}{9}\frac{}{16}\frac{}{26}\frac{}{7}\frac{}{24}$$

$$\frac{C}{25}\frac{C}{11}\frac{}{18}\frac{\bar{O}}{18}, \quad \frac{T}{9}\frac{}{16}\quad \frac{}{6}\frac{}{3}\frac{}{22}, \quad \frac{}{1}\frac{}{8}\frac{}{5}\frac{}{11}\quad \frac{}{8}\quad \frac{}{1}\frac{}{3}\frac{}{6}\frac{}{9}\frac{}{8}\frac{T}{5}\frac{}{11}$$

$$\frac{C}{25}\frac{C}{11}\frac{}{18}\frac{\bar{A}}{18}\frac{V}{2}\frac{\bar{I}}{}, \quad \frac{T}{9}\frac{}{16}\quad \frac{}{6}\frac{}{3}\frac{}{22}, \quad \frac{}{1}\frac{}{8}\frac{}{5}\frac{}{11}\quad \frac{}{8}\quad \frac{}{1}\frac{}{3}\frac{}{6}\frac{}{9}\frac{}{8}\frac{T}{5}\frac{}{11}$$

$$\frac{U}{3}\frac{R}{4}\frac{\bar{O}}{17}, \quad \frac{T}{9}\frac{}{16}\quad \frac{T}{9}\frac{}{8}\frac{}{5}\frac{}{11}\quad \frac{}{8}\frac{}{22}\quad \frac{T}{16}\frac{}{8}\frac{}{9}\frac{}{14}$$

$$\frac{\bar{O}}{15}\frac{}{8}\frac{}{1}\frac{}{22}, \quad \frac{T}{9}\frac{}{16}\quad \frac{C}{18}\frac{}{16}\frac{}{22}\frac{}{15}\frac{}{11}\frac{}{1}\frac{}{22}, \quad \frac{U}{25}\frac{}{4}\frac{}{22}\frac{}{3}\frac{}{6}\frac{}{14}$$

$$\frac{C}{18}\frac{}{16}\frac{}{22}\frac{C}{18}\frac{}{3}\frac{}{7}\frac{}{3}\frac{\bar{A}}{17}\frac{R}{11}, \quad \frac{T}{9}\frac{}{16}\quad \frac{R}{12}\frac{}{17}\frac{}{3}\frac{}{22}\frac{}{19}\quad \frac{T}{9}\frac{}{16}\frac{}{19}\frac{T}{11}\frac{}{9}\frac{}{14}\frac{R}{11}\frac{}{17},$$

$$\frac{U}{4}\frac{T}{22}\frac{}{3}\frac{}{9}\frac{}{11}$$

$$\frac{C}{18}\frac{}{16}\frac{}{22}\frac{R}{6}\frac{V}{11}\frac{\bar{O}}{17}\frac{}{2}, \quad \frac{T}{9}\frac{}{16}\quad \frac{}{5}\frac{}{11}\frac{}{11}\frac{}{25}, \quad \frac{R}{25}\frac{}{17}\frac{}{11}\frac{}{6}\frac{R}{11}\frac{}{17}\frac{V}{2}\frac{}{11}$$

$$\frac{}{3}\frac{\bar{U}}{15}\frac{}{11}\frac{}{13}, \quad (\underline{})\frac{}{1}\quad \frac{J}{20}\frac{U}{4}\frac{}{15}\frac{}{19}\frac{}{11}$$

$$\frac{T}{25}\frac{}{16}\frac{}{9}\frac{T}{11}\frac{}{6}\frac{\bar{A}}{9}\frac{T}{3}\frac{}{6}, \quad (\underline{})\quad \frac{W}{25}\frac{R}{16}\frac{}{23}\frac{}{11}\frac{}{17}$$

$$\frac{U}{8}\frac{C}{4}\frac{T}{18}\frac{}{9}\frac{\bar{O}}{17}\frac{R}{3}\frac{T}{9}\frac{}{8}\frac{}{6}, \quad (\underline{})\quad \frac{}{3}\frac{}{22}\frac{}{26}\frac{}{7}\frac{U}{4}\frac{}{11}\frac{}{22}\frac{C}{18}\frac{}{11}$$

$$\frac{U}{8}\frac{T}{4}\frac{}{9}\frac{R}{14}\frac{}{16}\frac{T}{17}\frac{}{3}\frac{}{9}\frac{}{24}$$

$$\frac{U}{8}\frac{C}{4}\frac{T}{18}\frac{\bar{O}}{9}\frac{R}{17}\frac{}{3}\frac{}{6}, \quad (\underline{})\quad \frac{C}{8}\frac{}{22}\frac{}{18}\frac{T}{11}\frac{}{6}\frac{R}{9}\frac{}{16}\frac{}{17}, \quad \frac{R}{16}\frac{}{17}\frac{}{3}\frac{}{19}\frac{}{3}\frac{}{22}\frac{T}{8}\frac{}{9}\frac{R}{16}\frac{}{17}$$

$$\frac{U}{6}\frac{}{4}\frac{}{25}\frac{}{25}\frac{R}{16}\frac{T}{17}\frac{}{9}\frac{R}{11}\frac{}{17}$$

$$\frac{}{7}\frac{}{11}\frac{}{13}, \quad (\underline{})\quad \frac{W}{7}\frac{}{8}\frac{}{23}, \quad \frac{C}{18}\frac{}{16}\frac{}{22}\frac{T}{9}\frac{R}{17}\frac{}{8}\frac{C}{18}\frac{T}{9}$$

$$\frac{\bar{E}}{7}\frac{}{19}\frac{}{3}\frac{}{6}, \quad (\underline{})\quad \frac{W}{7}\frac{}{8}\frac{}{23}, \quad \frac{C}{18}\frac{}{16}\frac{}{22}\frac{T}{9}\frac{R}{17}\frac{}{8}\frac{C}{18}\frac{T}{9}$$

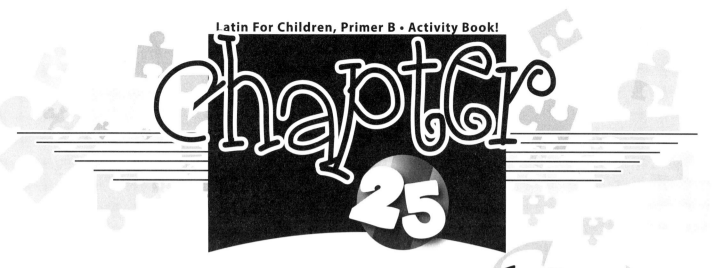

Chapter 25

Boxing

Looks like the little Latin elves left us a few boxes to fill in. Wanna have a crack at it?

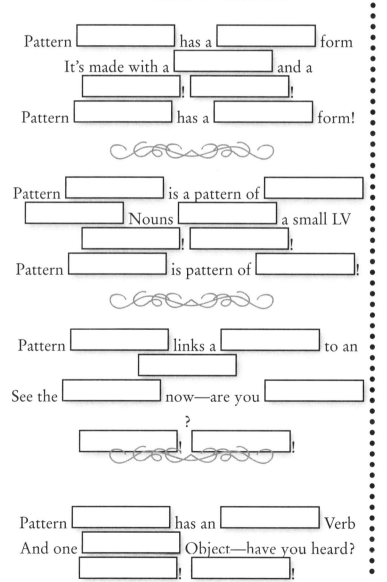

Pattern ☐ has a ☐ form

It's made with a ☐ and a

☐ ! ☐ !

Pattern ☐ has a ☐ form!

Pattern ☐ is a pattern of ☐

☐ Nouns ☐ a small LV

☐ ! ☐ !

Pattern ☐ is pattern of ☐ !

Pattern ☐ links a ☐ to an

See the ☐ now—are you

☐ ? ☐ !

Pattern ☐ has an ☐ Verb

And one ☐ Object—have you heard?

☐ ! ☐

Search Circle

```
G I G R R S A M K M O R S R A
S E R M O E Z R Z Z R Ō C C N
L X V M P R M A E D P R Y W V
I N V W S M D E P I G Ā K M G
U U L L M Ō I G X K T T N Q Z
Z L M A M N M I L I T I S F H
S A N G U I N I S F I Ō Q L S
C R O B I S O J G A D N B E L
H O I J Q I P E V I J I P K F
C N Q T U Y G N X M G S Z O V
S A L Ū T I S H O S T I S M J
E L Y M P N U V M O Z S P O K
H Q D G Ī L K V P Y E A A R X
P O U V W L A R N M Q N O T X
A B J I Q X E T O K U G A I A
L E L A T R O S R F E U E S F
T Z T T J I Y S Y Ō S I T Z B
V O N Ā L H S V I Z N S Ā B J
S A O C T U O M Y V N I S V Ō
M S U U S I X S R U A O S Q R
S G R S H K S K T M I B G T Ā
F A M R H L X O Q I Z U Q H T
F Q L U A U Y W G C S J D D I
L E A U O F B Y I Q Y K Z A O
G L J L S H H Y M D F Z B K R
```

EarthquaKE & RumblE!

That's right, we're juggling things around here! Can you fill in the questions since we've given you all the answers?

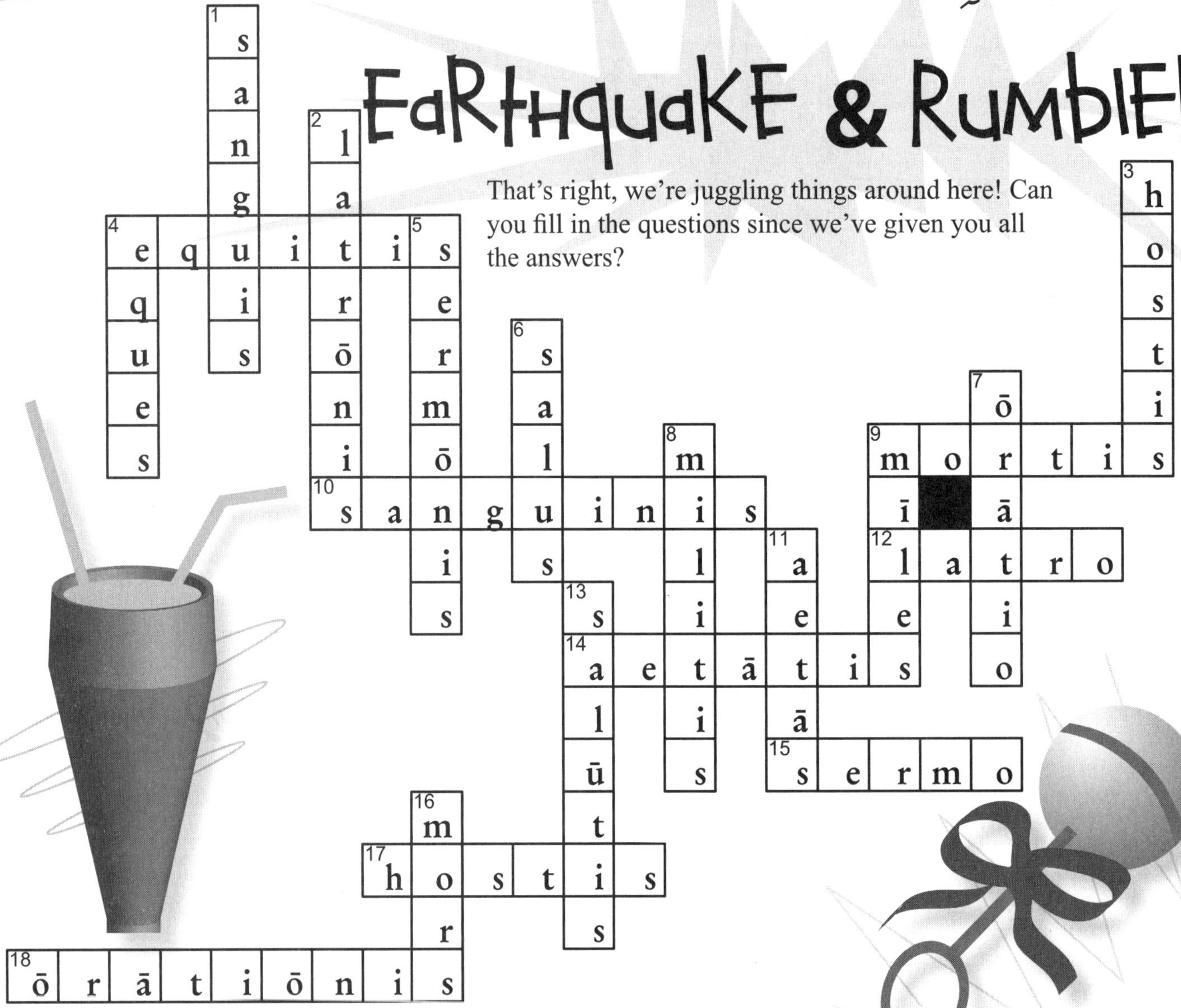

1 sanguis
2 latrōni
3 hostis
4 equitis
4 eques
5 sermōnis
6 salus
7 ōrātio
8 militis
9 mortis
9 mīles
10 sanguinis
11 aetās
12 latro
13 salūtis
14 aetātis
15 sermo
16 mors
17 hostis
18 ōrātiōnis

Across

4. ______________________________
9. ______________________________
10. ______________________________
12. ______________________________
14. ______________________________
15. ______________________________
17. ______________________________
18. ______________________________

Down

1. ______________________________
2. ______________________________
3. ______________________________
4. ______________________________
5. ______________________________
6. ______________________________
7. ______________________________
8. ______________________________
9. ______________________________
11. ______________________________
13. ______________________________
16. ______________________________

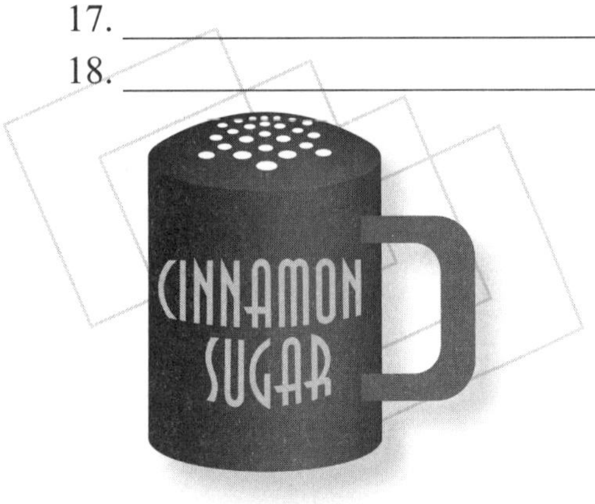

CINNAMON
SUGAR

What do these images have to do with the puzzle title?

GridWork

[tree]	[bulb]	ōrātiōnis	[tree]	[coffee]	[heart]	hostis	[cat]	sanguinis	[letter]
[fish]	[flower]	[cat]	[fish]	mors	[flower]	[car]	[heart]	[fish]	[tree]
hostis	[coffee]	salus	[letter]	[dog]	[flower]	[letter]	[coffee]	[letter]	salūtis
[dog]	[heart]	[car]	[tree]	[car]	equitis	[tree]	[cat]	[dog]	[bulb]
militis	[tree]	ōrātio	[flower]	[heart]	[heart]	[bulb]	[cat]	[flower]	[flower]
[heart]	[heart]	[coffee]	[coffee]	[car]	eques	[tree]	[car]	[coffee]	sermo
[cat]	aetās	[letter]	[dog]	latro	[fish]	[coffee]	[letter]	[heart]	[tree]
latrōnis	[fish]	[coffee]	[car]	[tree]	[car]	[bulb]	sermōnis	[fish]	[dog]
[bulb]	[coffee]	mīles	[cat]	mortis	[bulb]	[heart]	[car]	[letter]	aetātis
[dog]	[heart]	[letter]	[dog]	[cat]	sanguis	[heart]	[coffee]	[letter]	[coffee]

Follow these instructions carefully in order to find out which word is the *magic Latin word*. When you find it... ...if you find it... ...circle it!

1. Translate all the Latin words that are one block left of the cat — [cat].

2. Translate all the Latin words that are 2 blocks above or 2 blocks below the car — [car].

3. Translate the Latin that is one block up and to the right (upper diagonal right) from the heart — [heart].

4. Translate all Latin 4 squares to the left of the fish bones— [fish].

5. Translate all Latin words that touch (up/down, left/right & diagonals) the coffee cup ([coffee]) BUT not if the Latin word also touches a letter ([letter]).

6. Translate all Latin words that touch a letter ([letter]) BUT not if the letter ([letter]) touches an already translated Latin word.

7. Translate all Latin words that touch a Christmas Tree ([tree]) BUT only if the Latin word also touches a doggie ([dog]).

8. Circle the last word & translate!

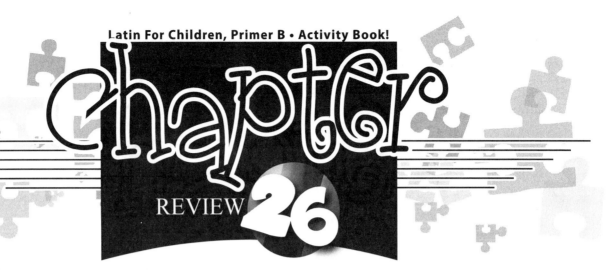

chapter
REVIEW 26

They're all here just waiting for you to **find** '**em**. Make sure you translate all the review words (all 90!) as you come across them.

```
A D X L B D C U D E S A Y L M O D O L Ō R I S U V
V F E Ū O F E X E Q B A E V N I S Ō L A B Ō R I S
S O F C I R L Ō C U A T L D E C L A R Ā T U M C K
M Ō X I L X E R L I E Q I Ū I N L I L Ā N W D C X
W Ī L S R A B I A T D P L M T F E U T U T T O E A
C S L I Y M R S R I I N E G Ō I I G X I S I L L E
L E J E S A Ā Ō S F A R S L R S C Ā L S L O E D
U V L T S F T T V A I A E D I F I C Ā V Ī A R B I
X I S E W F U B U Ī C V N O X J W S M R Ī B W R F
Y C Ō J B I M U E M Ā A O V E S T I S Y E Ō C Ā I
A T L A T R Ō N I S R R V L D E C L A R Ā R E V C
E O I M M Ā O W Ō E T M E U C L A B O R I N Ī Ō
T R S S O Ā O R B L Q I L O S N E D Y L N S O S D
Ā N V K R R U N E Y U S A Ū N T T L E L X X C C M
T D E N S E T J S V E F F W C T I Ā E N O C T I S
I E S E R M O I Q Ō S A F U E I I S T B T W I J P
S O T L A T R O S C A R I X D X S S G I R I S H V
I H I T I M O R L I Z T R O U X Ō R I S S Ō S O I
Q C S N E G Ā R E S A K M R M B S V L D O G K S C
Ō R Ā T I Ō N I S N B S Ō G Q O G E E A B T P T T
C P S F M Y A F F I R M Ā V Ī R N V R S B L P I Ō
N H S A V O L U N T Ā S A N G U I S I M T O W S R
Q L W R N E G Ā T U M R I V I C T O R C Ō I R O I
W Q A G V G A G D B O A Q D W R V L O W T N S S S
P R E T K U U W M K N W E V B W J Q R F Y Ō I K Y
Z U T I P U N I H Y T A M Ō R I S M L O V E R S G
M X Ā N N X O Q N Y I V Ō C I S A D E N S C X I O
H O S T I S X M S I S T C U C W J M S R M V R W S
X R X R O Z Ō J G Y S D E N T I S V O X T N V M K
Z K E N K E B L M X U A F B Q V B Z J R G E U U T
```

Mending Teddy

hārum

Plural
Gen.
Fem.

illō

hōc

illīus

illa

ille

illae

haec

hic

hās

illum

illōrum

huius

ilud

hī

huic

hīs

hanc

illī

illārum

illam

hōrum

illōs

Our old faithful teddy bear, "Jimichanga" has seen better days. Would you help us mend him by starting at the spool and adding the three (or more) missing components for each demonstrative pronoun? The first one is done for you.

Alphabet Soup

Pull up a chair. Have some soup!
These are words from this unit's review.
Can you sort out all the letters floating
about and rearrange them in order to find
out the lost phrase?
Oh,... did you want crackers?

ENGŌ, TO ENDY

⬜⬜⬜⬜⬜, ⬜⬜ ⬜⬜⬜⬜
　　　　　25　11 1

FIIEAŌDC, OT DUBLI, TREEC EISABTLHS

⬜⬜⬜⬜⬜⬜⬜⬜, ⬜⬜ ⬜⬜⬜⬜⬜⬜, ⬜⬜⬜⬜⬜ ⬜⬜⬜⬜⬜⬜⬜⬜
　　　　　26　24 3

CDLAŌER, OT ADEERCL

⬜⬜⬜⬜⬜⬜⬜, ⬜⬜ ⬜⬜⬜⬜⬜⬜⬜
　　　　　21　16　　23

RSA, (F) TRA, KSLLI

⬜⬜⬜, (⬜⬜) ⬜⬜⬜⬜, ⬜⬜⬜⬜⬜
　　　　　　　　27 10

LCISŪ, (F) LHGIT

⬜⬜⬜⬜⬜, (⬜⬜) ⬜⬜⬜⬜⬜
　　　　　12 14

XVO, (F) COEVI

⬜⬜⬜, (⬜⬜) ⬜⬜⬜⬜⬜
　　　20　　2

RPEĀCCE, TO NIS, KEAM A ESTIKAM

⬜⬜⬜⬜⬜⬜⬜, ⬜⬜ ⬜⬜⬜, ⬜⬜⬜⬜⬜⬜⬜⬜⬜
　　4　　　　19

MDŌAN, OT MDONNCE, NHSPUI

⬜⬜⬜⬜⬜, ⬜⬜ ⬜⬜⬜⬜⬜⬜⬜, ⬜⬜⬜⬜⬜
18　　　　　　　　　5

VCVNERĪOSĀ, OT KEPE, ERSEVEPR

⬜⬜⬜⬜⬜⬜⬜⬜⬜⬜, ⬜⬜ ⬜⬜⬜⬜, ⬜⬜⬜⬜⬜⬜⬜⬜
6

OITĀPSTTSE, (F) PEORW

⬜⬜⬜⬜⬜⬜⬜⬜⬜, (⬜⬜) ⬜⬜⬜⬜⬜
　　　　　　　　9

XEL, (F) LWA, TCCNROAT

⬜⬜⬜, (⬜⬜) ⬜⬜⬜, ⬜⬜⬜⬜⬜⬜⬜⬜
　　　8　　　17

EĪLSM, (C) ORSLDIE

⬜⬜⬜⬜⬜, (⬜⬜) ⬜⬜⬜⬜⬜⬜⬜
7

SULSA, (F) LEHHAT

⬜⬜⬜⬜⬜, (⬜⬜) ⬜⬜⬜⬜⬜
　　　　　13 22

AITSĀET, (F) AEG

⬜⬜⬜⬜⬜⬜, (⬜⬜) ⬜⬜⬜
　　　　　15

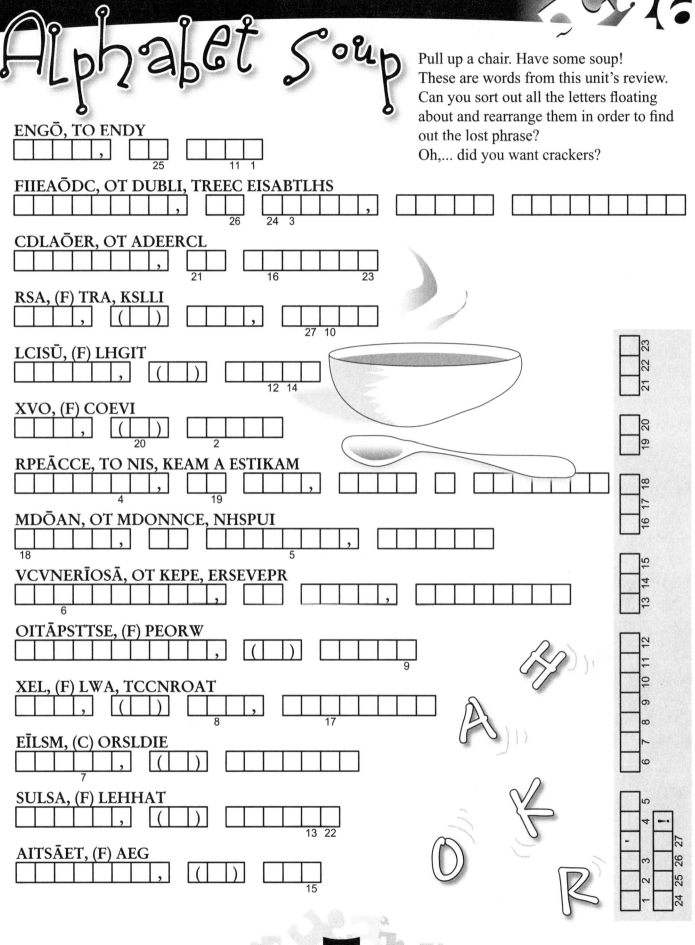

chapter 27

ignis!

With all your Fireman training, can you help save "Fred the fish" from this pet-shop blaze?! Complete the puzzle and you've put out the fire!

Editors Note: *Hmmm... now we might not be able to say that no animals where hurt...*

11. (f,i) ear
13. (m,i) limit, boundary
15. (f,i) bird
16. (m,i) limit, boundary
17. (f,i) bird
18. to fall
20. to run, hasten
21. (m) man, human be-ing
23. to write, engrave

Down
1. to trust, believe
2. to lead

4. to run, hasten
5. to run, hasten
7. to lead
10. to trust, believe
11. (f,i) ear
12. to write, engrave
14. (m,i) fire
18. to run, hasten
19. to write, engrave
21. (m) man, human being
22. (m,i) fire

Across
1. to fall
2. to lead
3. to lead
5. to fall
6. to trust, believe
8. to write, engrave
9. to fall
10. to trust, believe

For this puzzle you will need a firm grip on your leash... I mean, colored pens. You'll need to draw lines between the correct parts of **dūcō** but since there's enough lines and leashes already in this puzzle can you do it without touching another other lines?

dūcit

1st Person Bone

dūcitis

3rd Person Bone

dūcimus

Singular

dūcis

dūcō

Plural

2nd Person Bone

dūcunt

Did you know?

Ticket!

De integro

Repeat again from the start

For the Avis

Can you help "Skippy," the peanut butter loving bird, run around a bit (okay, birds don't run, yes, yes...)? She's been caged for quite some time and needs to stretch her wings.

scripsī

dūcō

auris

credere

cursum

fīnis

Start

cucurrī

currere

Finish

dūxī

homō

scrībō

cāsum

cadere

Found: _____, _____   _____, _____

_____, _____   _____,

chapter 28

RSPA ☐☐☐☐
　　　4

NDNAIIISTGŪM ☐☐☐☐☐☐☐☐☐☐☐☐☐
　　　　　　15

SPIED ☐☐☐☐☐
　　9　1

NISUDITLŪMIT ☐☐☐☐☐☐☐☐☐☐☐☐
　　　　24　　　　21

NĒSM ☐☐☐☐
　　23

ŌIATR ☐☐☐☐☐
　　3　22

MŌAGI ☐☐☐☐☐
　　6　27

ETSINM ☐☐☐☐☐☐
　2

SSCIIP ☐☐☐☐☐
　25　11

MIŪLTTUDŌ ☐☐☐☐☐☐☐☐☐
　　　　5

RISOB ☐☐☐☐☐
　14　10

RNAIITSO ☐☐☐☐☐☐☐☐
　　　7　　18

BSIRO ☐☐☐☐☐
　20　　　12

SITRPA ☐☐☐☐☐☐
　　26　8

NIIMIGAS ☐☐☐☐☐☐☐☐
　　　16

SPĒ ☐☐☐
　13

CPSSII ☐☐☐☐☐☐
　　　19

AŪNGTŌIDM ☐☐☐☐☐☐☐☐☐
　　　　17

Do You See Straight?

These words look like ordinary Latin words to me. Do they look that way to you? I mean, you do see that these are merely this weeks vocab, right?

A-huh. I was starting to wonder if you needed an eye exam.

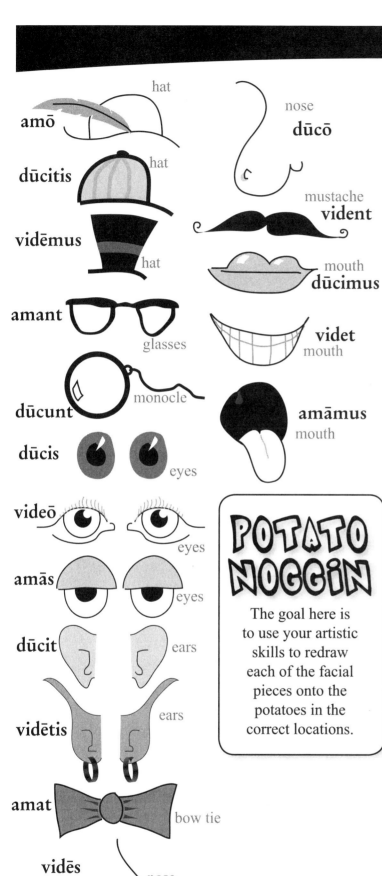

amō — hat

dūcitis — hat

vidēmus — hat

amant — glasses

dūcunt — monocle

dūcis — eyes

videō — eyes

amās — eyes

dūcit — ears

vidētis — ears

amat — bow tie

vidēs — nose

amātis — nose

dūcō — nose

vident — mustache

dūcimus — mouth

videt — mouth

amāmus — mouth

POTATO NOGGIN

The goal here is to use your artistic skills to redraw each of the facial pieces onto the potatoes in the correct locations.

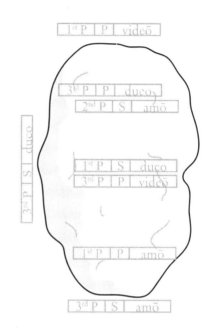

1st P | P | videō
3rd P | P | duco
2nd P | S | amō
3rd P | S | duco
1st P | S | duco
3rd P | P | videō
1st P | P | amō
3rd P | S | amō

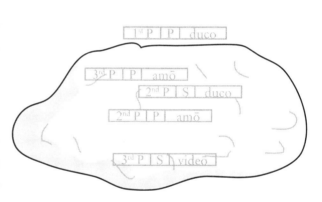

1st P | P | duco
3rd P | P | amō
2nd P | S | duco
2nd P | P | amō
3rd P | S | videō

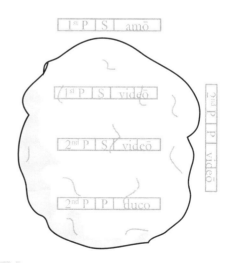

1st P | S | amō
1st P | S | videō
2nd P | S | videō
2nd P | P | videō
2nd P | P | duco

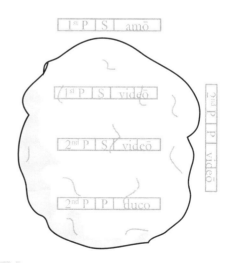

Pirate Gold!

Cap't Mol Vartin has hid his treasure and added false clues to the map to throw off all others. Think you can figure out which questions are the real ones and which one's aren't?

12. (f) image
13. (f) reckoning, account, calculation
13. (f) mind, understanding, reason
14. (f) circle, round thing, orb

Across

1. (m) lots of treasure
1. (f) large number, multitude
1. (x) as in "X" marks the spot
3. (f) greatness
3. (m,i) fish
3. man-eat'in shark (woman too!)
4. (f) image
4. (m) Argh, matie!
6. (f) circle, round thing, orb
6. (f) part, portion
7. (f) part, portion
7. starboard
7. (f) greatness
10. (m) foot
10. around the coconut grove
12. (f) circle, round thing, orb

Down

1. to walk/skip the plank
1. (f) large number, multitude
2. (f) reckoning, account, calculation
2. (m,i) fish
3. (f) greatness
3. (f) image
5. (m,i) fish
6. (m) foot
7. (m,i) fish
7. (m) swab the deck
8. (f) greatness
8. (f) circle, round thing, orb
9. (f) mind, understanding, reason
9. shiver me timbers (verb)
11. (f) mind, understanding, reason

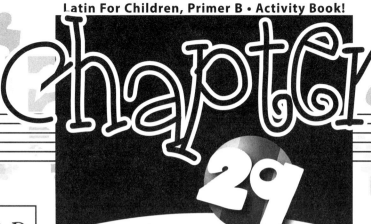

chapter 29

TightRope Walker

Can you find all
of this week's
vocabulary in the
two building that
help support the
tightrope walker?
Be careful not to
bump anything!

Found words
translated here:

_____ _____
_____ _____
_____ _____
_____ _____
_____ _____
_____ _____
_____ _____
_____ _____
_____ _____
_____ _____
_____ _____
_____

Left grid:

```
S S D P D
A U S Ō O
P R U N S
Ō R E J J
N Ē R R S
Ō C Ē E S
D T X W U
Ī U Ī G R
C M O Q G
E V Ī V Ō
R Ī Ī J Q
E V B X P
L E U V Ī
E R M O Z
M E O W D
R R G S D
Z Z E U I
W A E R C
P V Z G T
D J I E U
E Ī O R B
G Q X E R
J P Q Ī S
P O S U Ī
Y S E J A
P I S L Y
M T G Q P
L U C I W
T M A Z V
D Ī C O G
```

Right grid:

```
D L V C L
P I I R A
P T N I T
Q O C M U
Q R E E S
Z I R N Y
K S E K T
V I N C Ō
N Ō M E N
L V R F E
Ō Ī Ī G F
R A T C V
I I N U Ī
S D Ō V S
C K M I L
K C I C O
J O N T C
U R I U O
C P S M R
R O V E P
I R D T U
M I M P S
I S T F V
N F L L Ī
I L A Ū C
S Ū T M T
Q M E I U
Y E R N M
L N I I B
Ō S S S N
```

Mow the Lawn

Draw one continuous line from the mower across the yard, circling only the GENITIVE, ACCUSATIVE & ABLATIVE rocks.

It's raining so heavily that it's raining—well, you get the point. Would you be so kind as to write the 3rd declension neuter endings under the correct umbrellas and get them out from the miserable weather?

CATS & DOGS

Did you know?

Ticket!
Ita est
Yes, it is so

SWISS CHEESY

Yeah, YOU fill in the holes. Got it? One last thing... this puzzle only has a few of this week's words.

Used-Cheese Salesman

cheesy

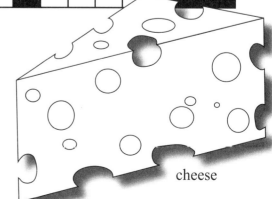

cheese

Chapter 30

Word Crossing

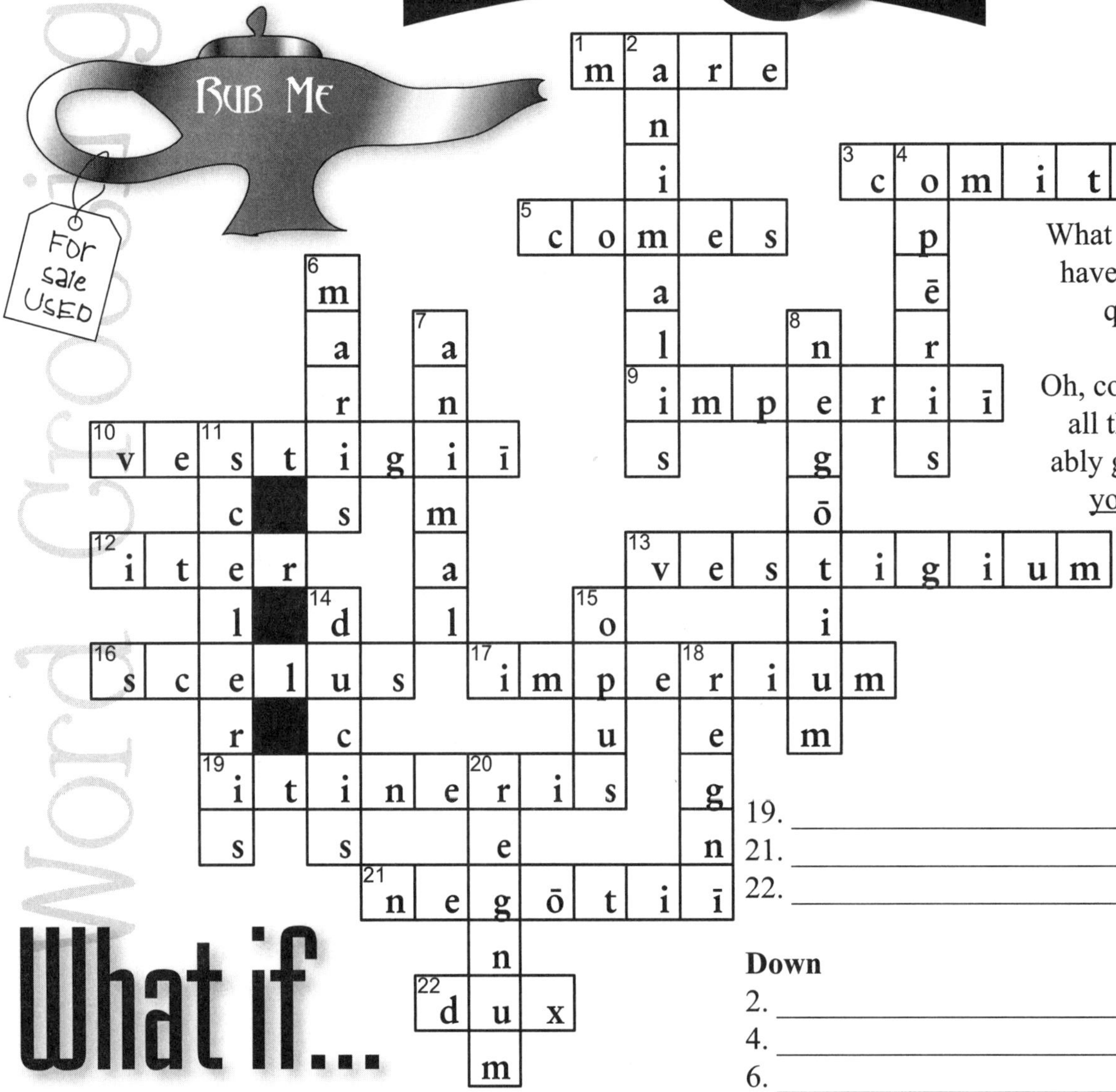
Rub Me
For sale USED
1 mare
2 animalis
3 comitis
4 operis
5 comes
6 maris
7 animal
8 negōtium
9 imperiī
10 vestigiī
11 sceleris
12 iter
13 vestigium
14 ducis
15 opus
16 scelus
17 imperium
18 regnī
19 itineris
20 regnum
21 negōtiī
22 dux

What if you made a wish to have the answers to all the quizzes, tests & puzzle and it came true?! Oh, come on, it wouldn't be all that great. You'd probably get a puzzle that made you fill in the questions. Then where would you be?

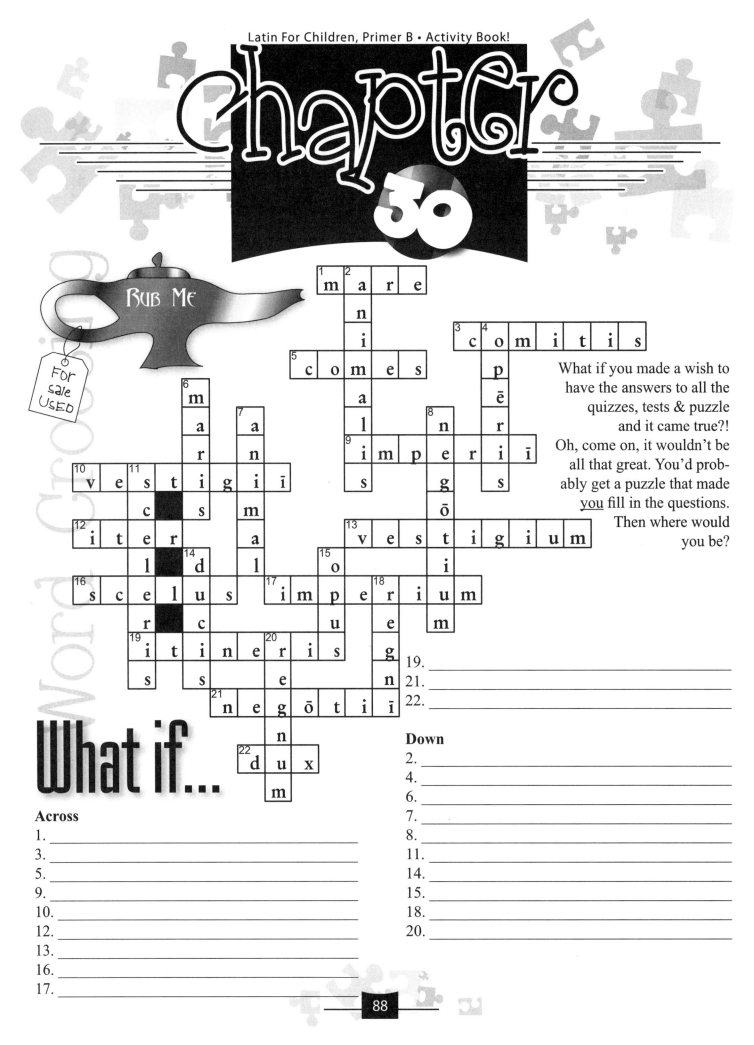

What if...

Across

1. ____________________
3. ____________________
5. ____________________
9. ____________________
10. ____________________
12. ____________________
13. ____________________
16. ____________________
17. ____________________
19. ____________________
21. ____________________
22. ____________________

Down

2. ____________________
4. ____________________
6. ____________________
7. ____________________
8. ____________________
11. ____________________
14. ____________________
15. ____________________
18. ____________________
20. ____________________

CANDY Country!

Hmm... We found this old game at a yard sale. The rules say that you can play it with either one dice or to simply start on the first square. It seems to involve some 3rd declension neuter I-stems. Not so sure about the rest of it. I don't think this was ever the board-game-success that that other candy game is.

Start

Dative Singular
_____
move forward 3

Lost tooth on Jawbreaker
_____
back to START

You are Sugar Plum Fairy's Fav!
_____
roll die

Mother Sugar Load Found!
_____
roll die

Cavity Creeps!
_____
move back 1

Accusative Singular
_____
go forward 5

GumDrop Alley. Mugged by bad Candy
_____
move back 2

Ice Cream melts!
_____
move back 3

Genitive Plural
_____
go forward 1

Ablative Singular
_____
go forward 4

Singular -ium
_____
go forward 2

Candy Toothpaste loses market shares
_____
move back 2

Accusative Plural
_____
go forward 2

Licorice Soda Pop. What were you thinking?!
_____
START over

Finish

Popcorn Ball rolls off the table and out the door.
_____
move back 2

Invent Cotton Candy with Substance!
_____
move forward 1

CupCake Collision. Exchange insurance cards
_____
move back 2

Candy Mint Makes Breath Bad!
_____
move back 1

Receive Valentine Hearts!
_____
roll die

Ablative Plural
_____
move forward 5

You get Candy Corns on your feet
_____
move back 1

Sugar Overload!
_____
move back 2

Singular -is
_____
move forward 3

Hard Candy. Loose Tooth.
_____
move back 2

Genitive Singular
_____
go forward 4

Lollipop Lane Realestate Tax
_____
move back 2

Nominative Singular
_____
move forward 3

Pudding Swamp. Lose spoon.
_____
move back 3

Creme Brule - Perfectly made!
_____
roll die

Taffy Laughy BONUS!
_____
move forward 1

Dative Plural
_____
move forward 3

Invent Candy Zipper!
_____
roll die

Sour Sweets Construction Zone
_____
move back 2

Lollipop in Sister's Hair
_____
move back 1

Bubble Gum on Shoe
_____
move back 1

Nominative Plural
_____
move forward 4

Candy Card

A	B	C	D	E	F	G	H	I	J	K	L	M	N	O	P	Q	R	S	T	U	V	W	X	Y	Z
		14							13	26	16		15				24	19		11				2	

Scelus! Scelus!

Someone stole most of the letters that make up the Latin words to the left. Can you find 'em again?

Did you know?

Ticket!

Ut humiliter opinor

In my humble opinion

Left column cryptogram:

```
      R
22  6 24 10

  O    U  S
 15    9 11 19

      R     S
22  6 24  3 19

 S  C    L  U  S
19 14 10 16 11 19

            R     S
 3  7  3  4 10 24  3 19

            R     U
 3 22  9 10 24  3 11 22

 O    Ē R     S
15  9 24  3 19

            R
 3  7 10 24

       Ō     Ī
 4 10  1  7  3

    S              U
21 10 19  7  3  1  3 11 22

    U
20 11 17

            R     Ī
 3 22  9 10 24  3

       Ō     U
 4 10  1  7  3 11 22

    S           Ī
21 10 19  7  3  1  3

 R           U
24 10  1  4 11 22

 R              Ī
24 10  1  4

 C  O        S
14 15 22 10 19

                L
 6  4  3 22  6 16

    U  C     S
20 11 14  3 19
```

IF NEEDED

(n, i) sea
(n) a work, a labor
(n, i) sea
(n) crime
(n) journey, road
(n) command, order, power.
(n) a work, a labor
(n) journey, road
business, occupation
footprint, trace, track
power, rule, realm
(m) leader, ruler, commander
(m) companion
(n, i) animal
power, rule, realm
(m) leader, ruler, commander
business, occupation
footprint, trace, track

chapter
REVIEW 31

ROUTE 66

Hit the Highway

```
D O U Y T R V S F O S O C O O X T J Z F
Ū P I S C I S Ī C F Z C R A I P F I L Ī
C S V Y Z Y J B C R N C E B D Y L P V N
E U Ī L A O Q H Y T I M E L I Ō Ū A H I
R R C S U R G E R E U P A C U S M R O S
E G Ī U N E G Ō T I Ī M T G I S E T M P
Ō Ō K Q R P G L Ī T U S Q U N D N I I E
S P I M F R O C U R R E R E M I Ī S N D
X Ō M I A C Ī S M D V L X N S M T Y I I
J N P I U R P S U U U I W O I U O Ū S S
I E E T K E E K L Ī X X D U C T U M D L
M R R E J D C N T V Ī V E R E Ō R I S Ō
A E I R T I N H I D A Z A I C Z F D I T
G S Ī F R D Ō G T U I U X L G E I Ī Z
I S E Y K Ī M A Ū S R C R P A N K C I C
N S C U L W E W D L J K T I P T I O N R
I V C E V A N Q Ō A V I S U S N E S E E
S B Ī R L I T O L D G Q T G M I O R R D
W K N V Ī E M U L T I T Ū D I N I S I Ō
C U R R Ō B R H S A X C O R P O R I S S
O R B I S A Ō I U N R A T I Ō D R G A D
X V V H C J X M S I V R N H T V C N B Ū
G F Q O R R I M U M Z U E Z U R W I U C
R E G N Ī T E M D A T M V G P K O S R Ō
B L N V N H H D Ē L T P V S N S F V R G
S C R Ī B E R E E N D Ī X Ī O U C C R O
P I X E Y W Q H D R S P Ē S D N M Q J U
V F V E S T I G I Ī E J X I P W S F X D
O P Ē R I S Q Q Q C R I M E N F Ī N I S
D C C C P F H V O J K J X X C F N P L G
```

Ready to take a drive? There are 66 review words tucked into this puzzle. Just how many can you find before you need to take a break at a rest stop?
More importantly, how many can you translate once you find them?

Number found: _____

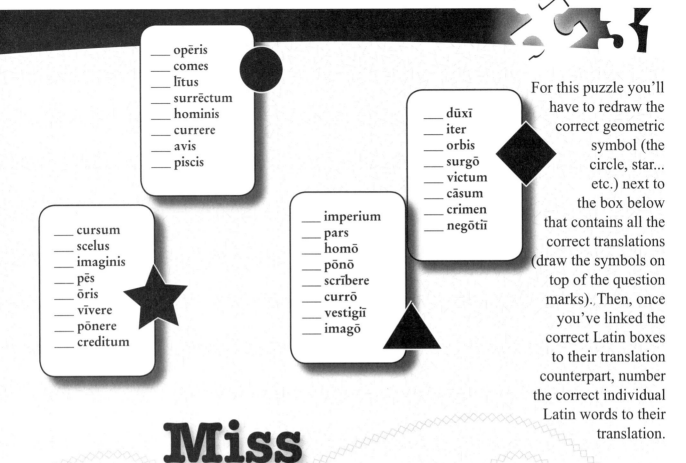

___ opēris
___ comes
___ lītus
___ surrēctum
___ hominis
___ currere
___ avis
___ piscis

___ cursum
___ scelus
___ imaginis
___ pēs
___ ōris
___ vīvere
___ pōnere
___ creditum

___ imperium
___ pars
___ homō
___ pōnō
___ scrībere
___ currō
___ vestigiī
___ imagō

___ dūxī
___ iter
___ orbis
___ surgō
___ victum
___ cāsum
___ crimen
___ negōtiī

For this puzzle you'll have to redraw the correct geometric symbol (the circle, star... etc.) next to the box below that contains all the correct translations (draw the symbols on top of the question marks). Then, once you've linked the correct Latin boxes to their translation counterpart, number the correct individual Latin words to their translation.

Miss Match

6. (m) man, human being
4. (m) companion
2. (n) shore, beach
8. to run, hasten
5. (m,i) fish
3. to rise, get up
7. (f,i) bird
1. (n) a work, a labor

3. (n) crime
7. (n) mouth, face
8. to run, hasten
2. to live
6. (m) foot
4. to trust, believe
5. to put, place
1. (f) image

5. (f) part, portion
8. to write, engrave
4. (f) image
2. command, order, power
3. to run, hasten
7. footprint, trace, track
6. (m) man, human being
1. to put, place

1. to rise, get up
2. (n) crime, accusation
8. (f) circle, round thing, orb
3. to lead
7. to conquer
4. to fall
6. (n) journey, road
5. business, occupation

These words below aren't Latin words scrambled up, they are actually the English translations. Can you figure out what scrambled English words they are, then translate them.

SOMETHING OLD, SOMETHING NEW...

ftaoll

ttboelriuesvte

hraustteonn

letaod

ewrntgoirtaeve

bloiumndairty

mlnuuarmltibtgeurdee

cirrtoohuicnldernbg

tpouptlace

urpitgoseet

Editor's Note:
Isn't there supposed to be something blue here as well? Do we have color in the budget?

alawboorark

joruoranedy

ordceopmrmoanwedr

boucscuinpeastiosn

ftortroatapcrcienkt

prruoelweaelrm

rluleecaormdmaenderr

HINTS:

Cover these up if you don't want to use them.

dux, ducis
regnum, regni
vestigium, vestigii
negotium, negotii
imperium, imperii
iter, itineris
opus, operis
surgo, surgere, surrexi, surrectum

pono, ponere, posui, positum
orbis, orbis
multitudo, multitudinis
finis, finis
scribo, scribere, scripsi, scriptum
duco, ducere, duxi, ductum
curro, currere, cucurri, cursum
credo, credere, credidi, creditum
cado, cadere, cecidi, casum

chapter
REVIEW 32

whopper crossword puzzle!*

We've included a crossword puzzle that involves every single vocabulary word that you've learned in the **Latin For Children, Primer B** text book.

This puzzle is so big that you might want to assemble it and begin filling in the answers BEFORE you get to the final review chapter. If you do that, just skip over the questions that you don't know and slowly work away at the puzzle. Remember, it's a whopper! so don't expect to have it done overnight.

RULES:

Remember the old "weeds" crossword puzzles where you had to figure out which question were the real ones? Well, this puzzle is similar but not exactly the same. You have to read all the crossword questions (they are all used!) but then YOU have to figure out with of the seven crossword sections (sub-sets of the whole puzzle) that they belong to. Oooo, sounds like a puzzle inside a puzzle!

Did you know?

Ticket!

Die dulci freure

Have a nice day

* Some assembly required.

INSTRUCTIONS:

1. Cut out each puzzle page (15 total) along their outer grey lines.

2. Lay out the pages <u>face up</u> (5 across, 3 down). Use the large grey letters on the back of each puzzle page as reference only:

A	B	C	D	E
F	G	H	I	J
K	L	M	N	O

3. Carefully align each page to each other (there is no puzzle overlap!). Use clear tape to attach the separate puzzle pages into one poster sized puzzle.

4. Use pen or permanent marker especially on puzzle answer blocks underneath the clear tape.

5. Enjoy & Learn!

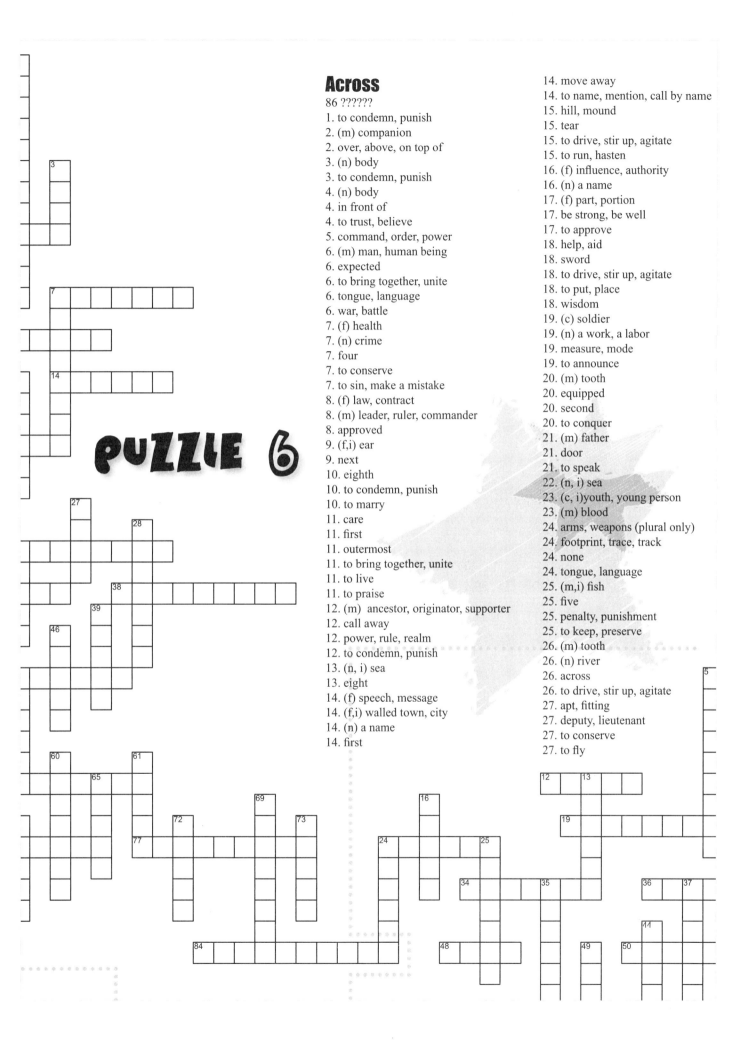

Across

86 ??????

1. to condemn, punish
2. (m) companion
2. over, above, on top of
3. (n) body
3. to condemn, punish
4. (n) body
4. in front of
4. to trust, believe
5. command, order, power
6. (m) man, human being
6. expected
6. to bring together, unite
6. tongue, language
6. war, battle
7. (f) health
7. (n) crime
7. four
7. to conserve
7. to sin, make a mistake
8. (f) law, contract
8. (m) leader, ruler, commander
8. approved
9. (f,i) ear
9. next
10. eighth
10. to condemn, punish
10. to marry
11. care
11. first
11. outermost
11. to bring together, unite
11. to live
11. to praise
12. (m) ancestor, originator, supporter
12. call away
12. power, rule, realm
12. to condemn, punish
13. (n, i) sea
13. eight
14. (f) speech, message
14. (f,i) walled town, city
14. (n) a name
14. first

14. move away
14. to name, mention, call by name
15. hill, mound
15. tear
15. to drive, stir up, agitate
15. to run, hasten
16. (f) influence, authority
16. (n) a name
17. (f) part, portion
17. be strong, be well
17. to approve
18. help, aid
18. sword
18. to drive, stir up, agitate
18. to put, place
18. wisdom
19. (c) soldier
19. (n) a work, a labor
19. measure, mode
19. to announce
20. (m) tooth
20. equipped
20. second
20. to conquer
21. (m) father
21. door
21. to speak
22. (n, i) sea
23. (c, i)youth, young person
23. (m) blood
24. arms, weapons (plural only)
24. footprint, trace, track
24. none
24. tongue, language
25. (m,i) fish
25. five
25. penalty, punishment
25. to keep, preserve
26. (m) tooth
26. (n) river
26. across
26. to drive, stir up, agitate
27. apt, fitting
27. deputy, lieutenant
27. to conserve
27. to fly

PUZZLE 6

28. (n) shore, beach
28. star
28. to fly
28. to help
29. (n, i) animal
29. injury, injustice
29. people
29. to run, hasten
30. (f) image
30. (n) journey, road
30. oar
31. married
31. power, rule, realm
32. money
32. to declare
32. to write, engrave
32. within
33. (f) influence, authority
33. (f,i) bird
33. (m) old man
33. (n) mouth, face
33. under
34. (n) crime
34. people
34. the other
34. to lead
35. (m) father
35. (n) a work, a labor
35. into
36. duty, respect
36. to lead
36. wine
37. (c) soldier
37. (f) law, contract
37. penalty, punishment
38. (f) speech, message
38. hour
38. through
38. to ask or question
38. to bring together, unite
38. to owe, ought
39. living
39. on account of
39. to keep, preserve
40. shape, beauty
41. to declare

41. to equip
41. to live
43. (f) mind, understanding, reason
43. (m) pain, anguish, sorrow
43. beautiful
43. fight
43. help, aid
44. (f) part, portion
44. dead
44. king
44. move
44. to build, erect establish
45. one
45. to fly
45. to terrify, frighten
46. select, adopt
46. to sin, make a mistake
47. (m,i) limit, boundary
47. tongue, language
48. (m,i) fish
48. hour
48. last
48. outside
48. to strengthen, assert, affirm
49. duty, respect
49. hole
49. to condemn, punish
49. to run, hasten
50. (c) stranger, foreigner, enemy (of one's country)
50. (m) the sun
50. messenger
50. to respond
51. I expect
51. one
51. to marry
51. to sin, make a mistake
52. (f) will
52. flame
53. certain
53. to speak
54. (f) night
54. (f) power
54. apt, fitting
54. to conserve
55. (f) power

55. (m,i) limit, boundary
55. in front of
55. move away
56. (m) judge
56. middle
56. pebble
56. three
56. to bring together, unite
57. certain
58. (f) death
58. (m) brother
58. it (nominative or accusative case)
59. (m) judge
59. little bag
59. move away
60. be strong, be well
60. I prayed
60. move
61. effort, services
61. river bank
61. ten
63. along
63. the other
63. to help
63. to respond
64. (f) mother
64. to help
64. to rise, get up
64. to sin, make a mistake
65. (f,i) clothing, garment
65. be strong, be well
65. flame
65. little bag
66. (m) victor

PUZZLE 2

66. dead
66. rose
66. to announce
66. to conquer
67. measure, mode
67. ninth
67. to terrify, frighten
68. equal
68. him (accusative case)
68. to deny
68. to write, engrave
69. fault
69. life
69. nature, birth
70. (m,i) fire
70. thanks
70. with
71. hundred
71. none
71. to marry
72. cause
72. out of
72. shape, beauty
72. to save
72. to sin, make a mistake
73. rose
73. to bring together, unite
74. (m) judge
74. care
74. third
74. to fall
74. to praise
74. to terrify, frighten
75. equal

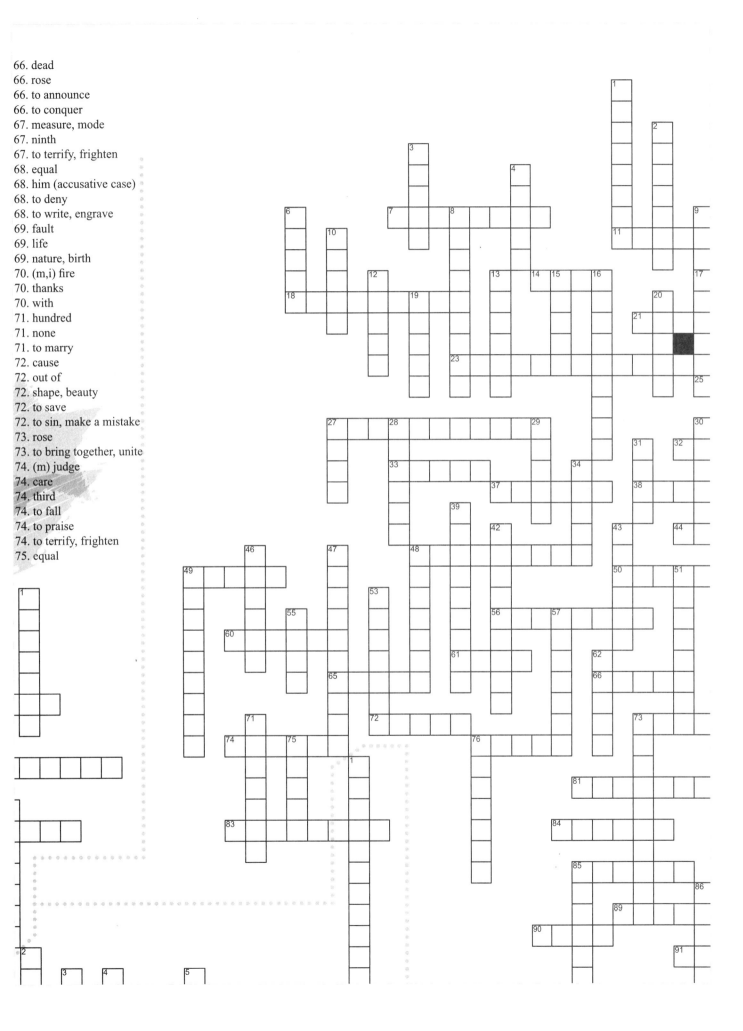

PUZZLE 4

Latin For Children, ?

master REViEW

The goal
QUES
PUZZL
the puz
finish t

PUZZLE 7

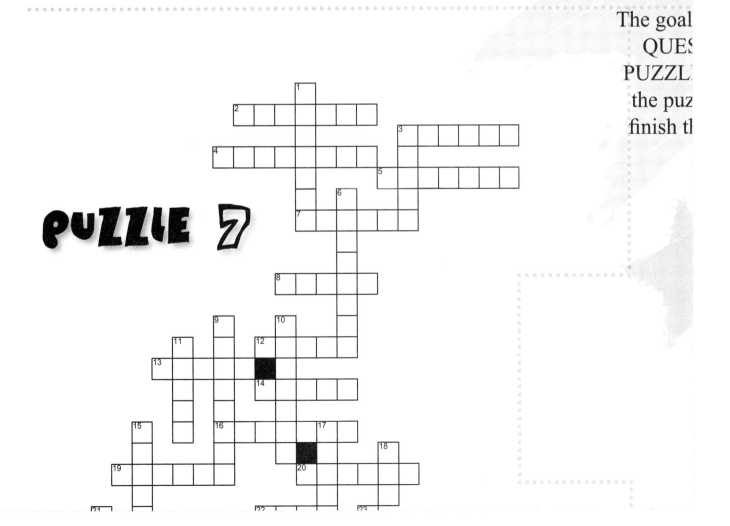

PUZZLE WHOPPER

here is to figure out which
STION goes with which
E (no. 1 thru 7) then fill in
zle accordingly. Can you
his whopper of a puzzle?!

PUZZLE 1

PUZZLE 5

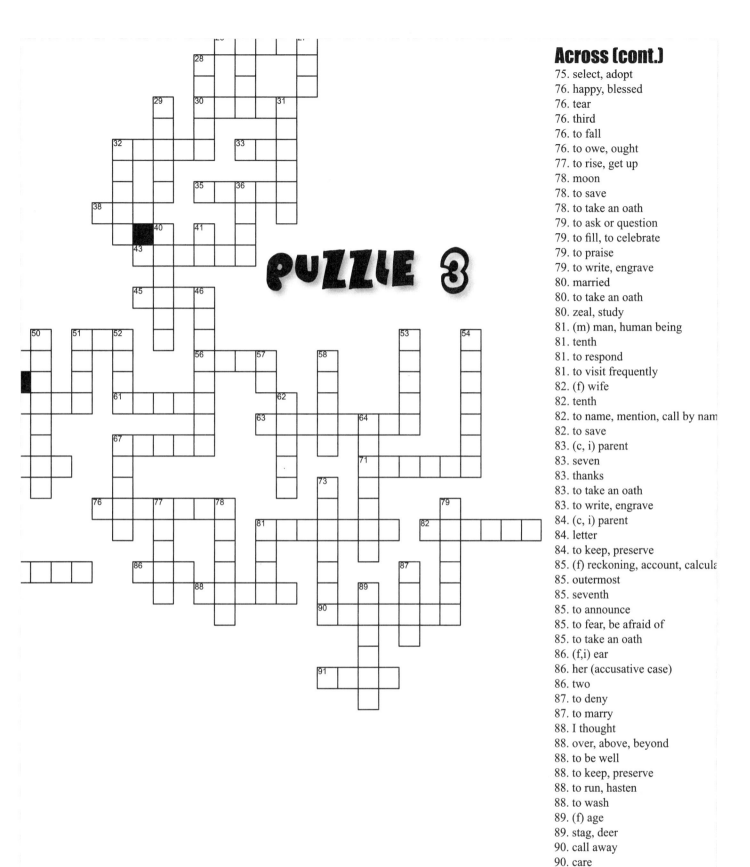

75. select, adopt
76. happy, blessed
76. tear
76. third
76. to fall
76. to owe, ought
77. to rise, get up
78. moon
78. to save
78. to take an oath
79. to ask or question
79. to fill, to celebrate
79. to praise
79. to write, engrave
80. married
80. to take an oath
80. zeal, study
81. (m) man, human being
81. tenth
81. to respond
81. to visit frequently
82. (f) wife
82. tenth
82. to name, mention, call by nam
82. to save
83. (c, i) parent
83. seven
83. thanks
83. to take an oath
83. to write, engrave
84. (c, i) parent
84. letter
84. to keep, preserve
85. (f) reckoning, account, calcula
85. outermost
85. seventh
85. to announce
85. to fear, be afraid of
85. to take an oath
86. (f,i) ear
86. her (accusative case)
86. two
87. to deny
87. to marry
88. I thought
88. over, above, beyond
88. to be well
88. to keep, preserve
88. to run, hasten
88. to wash
89. (f) age
89. stag, deer
90. call away
90. care
90. none

90. second
90. to put, place
91. I approved
91. move
91. to fly
91. to owe, ought
92. (c, i) young person (age 20-40)
92. equal
92. to take an oath
93. (f, i) clan, tribe
93. to declare
94. to deny

Down

1. (f) large number, multitude
1. (n) shore, beach
1. after
1. i) young person (age 20-40)
1. to help or manage
1. to wash
2. memory
2. number, measure
2. to be well
2. to fly
2. to lead
3. (m) companion
3. I approve
3. near
3. sister
3. to condemn, punish
3. to live
3. wife
4. (c, i) citizen
4. her (accusative case)
4. last
4. to bring together, unite
4. to keep, preserve
5. (f) large number, multitude
5. (m) labor, work
5. angle
5. I expected
5. near
5. select, adopt
6. (f, i) ship
6. deputy, lieutenant
6. footprint, trace, track
7. (m) talk, conversation, discourse
7. fourth
7. move away
7. next
8. (m) ancestor, originator, supporter
8. fourth
8. it (nominative or accusative case)
8. sentence
9. (n) crime, accusation

9. thanks
9. to build, erect establish
9. to save
9. two
10. (m) ancestor, originator, supporter
10. (m) pain, anguish, sorrow
10. business, occupation
10. eighth
10. fault, blame, sin
10. to pray
11. (n)side
12. (m) old man
12. dead
12. oar
13. (m, i) mountain
13. eye
13. number, measure
13. sleep
13. to live
14. (m, i) mountain
14. help, aid
15. (m) fear
15. (m) king
15. command, order, power
15. to praise
16. (f) reckoning, account, calculation
16. sentence
16. sword
16. to ask or question
16. wine
17. (n) journey, road
17. arms, weapons
17. shape, beauty
17. to visit frequently
18. (m) leader, ruler, commander
18. to help or manage
18. to sin, make a mistake
19. below
19. to condemn, punish
19. to fear, be afraid of
20. (f) law, contract
20. (f, i) ship
20. shape, beauty
21. (m) labor, work
21. (n) mouth, face
21. ninth
21. strange
22. (f) greatness
22. (f) voice
22. thousand
22. to announce
22. to help or manage
22. to sit
23. (m) ancestor, originator, supporter
23. (n) crime, accusation
23. fight
23. living

23. to rise, get up
23. tongue, language
24. citizenship, state, commonwealth
24. to bring together, unite
24. to put, place
24. to wash
25. (n) river
25. call away
25. fourth
25. to order or command
26. (m,i) fire
26. effort, services
26. strange
26. to strengthen, assert, affirm
27. (f,i) bird
27. (n) side
27. hole
27. six
28. around
28. to rise, get up
28. to sit
29. (f) light
29. (f) mother
29. (n, i) animal
29. beyond
30. moon
30. to declare
30. to drive, stir up, agitate
30. to sit
31. (m) judge
31. to ask or question
31. to sin, make a mistake
31. to sit
31. up to
32. (f) health
32. between
32. business, occupation
32. married
32. strange
33. (f) influence, authority
33. certain
33. hour
34. (f) wife
34. battle
34. be strong, be well
35. (f) greatness
35. tear
35. to order or command
35. to sin, make a mistake
36. (m) love
36. before
36. I equip
36. to laugh, smile
37. from, by
37. messenger
37. trial, legal investigation
39. (f) circle, round thing, orb

39. help, aid
39. past
39. to strengthen, assert, affirm
40. (f) will
40. (m) brother
40. fifth
40. prayed
40. to put, place
41. in, on
41. move
41. to laugh, smile
42. (c) leader, first one, prince
42. second
42. to build, erect establish
42. to name, mention, call by name
42. to speak
42. zeal, study
43. beautiful
43. stag, deer
43. to condemn, punish
44. luxury, extravagance
45. (f) age
45. luxury, extravagance
45. next
46. fault, blame, sin
46. last
46. seventh
46. to fall
47. battle
47. happy, blessed
47. to bring together, unite
47. to conserve
48. (f) voice
48. beautiful
48. to strengthen, assert, affirm
49. (f) citizenship, state, commonwealth
49. first
49. memory
50. (c) stranger, foreigner, enemy (of one's country)
50. injury, injustice
50. seventh
51. leader, first one, prince
51. one
51. to speak
52. (f) circle, round thing, orb
52. among,by, at, near
52. trial, legal investigation
52. wisdom
53. (f) light
53. angle
53. cause
53. face-to-face with
53. tear
54. (c, i) citizen
54. (f) power
54. fifth

54. husband
55. (f, i) clan, tribe
55. call away
55. to help or manage
56. select, adopt
56. to keep, preserve
57. (f) night
57. (m) horseman, knight, equestrian
57. pebble
57. to wash
57. to, toward
58. (f) death
58. nature, birth
58. ninth
58. to take an oath
59. (m) foot
59. sleep
59. to think
60. door
60. to keep, preserve
60. to trust, believe
61. (m) foot
61. living
61. to take an oath
62. (f) mind, understanding, reason
62. (f,i) walled town, city
62. happy, blessed
62. him (accusative case)
62. to build, erect establish
62. war, battle
63. (m) the sun
63. to conquer
64. tenth
64. to expect
65. (m) horseman, knight, equestrian
65. flame
65. I think
65. sixth
66. against
66. middle
67. door
67. nine
67. to fill, to celebrate
67. to keep, preserve
68. from, concerning, about
68. to laugh, smile
69. (f) power
69. (m) robber, mercenary
69. before, on behalf of
70. thanks
70. thought
70. to fly
70. youth, young person
71. (m) fear
71. (m) robber, mercenary
71. money
72. flame

72. to trust, believe
73. (f) image
73. door
73. fifth
73. I pray
73. to respond
74. the other
75. (m) victor
75. river bank
75. three
75. to lead
76. (f) art, skill
76. to owe, ought
77. (f) law, contract
77. hour
77. to deny
77. to order or command
77. to the extent of
78. I equipped
78. letter
78. sixth
78. to conquer
79. life
79. sixth
80. third
80. to fall
80. to fear, be afraid of
80. to take an oath
81. to help
81. to order or command
81. two
82. (m) talk, conversation, discourse
82. eye
83. (m) blood
83. to name, mention, call by name
84. hill, mound
84. skill
84. star
85. to terrify, frighten
86. outermost
86. to laugh, smile
87. (f) sister
87. apt, fitting
87. to trust, believe
87. without
89. (f) influence, authority
89. (f,i) clothing, garment
89. care
89. eighth
89. fault
90. to fly
91. to fly

93

94

Tricky Words
(more practice needed):

Did you know?

Ticket!

Flamma fumo est proxima

Flame follows smoke.
There's no smoke without a fire.
(Plautus)

ANSWERS Ahead!

Do ***NOT***
proceed forward
unless, of course,
you're looking
for the answers.

ANSWER  KEY

Chapter 1

(Crossword solution)

- 1. ornātum
- 2. extrema
- 3. probō
- 5. putō
- 7. posterus
- 9. orō
- 11. putāre
- 13. exspectāre
- 15. exspectātum
- 17. mortuus
- 20. ornāvī
- 21. vīva
- 22. vīvus
- 23. probātum
- 25. extremus
- 26. putāvī
- 27. probāre

	1ST declension		2ND declension (m)		2ND declension (m)		2ND declension (n)	
	S	P	S	P	S	P	S	P
Nominative	-a	-ae	-us	-ī	-um	-ī	-um	-a
Genitive	-ae	-ārum	-ī	-ōrum	-ī	-ōrum	-ī	-ōrum
Dative	-ae	-īs	-ō	-īs	-ō	-īs	-ō	-īs
Accusative	-am	-ās	-um	-ōs	-um	-ōs	-um	-a
Ablative	-ā	-īs	-ō	-īs	-ō	-īs	-ō	-īs

CODE BREAKER

probātis -- present, plural, 2nd person • orant -- present, plural, 3rd person

exspectābit -- future, singular, 3rd person • probābunt -- future, plural, 3rd person

putābāmus -- imperfect, plural, 1st person

(Word search with word list):

orō, I pray
orāre, to pray
orāvī, I prayed
orātum, prayed
ornō, I equip
ornāre, to equip
ornāvī, I equipped
ornātum, equipped
exspectō, I expect
exspectāre, to expect
exspectāvī, I expected
exspectātum, expected
putō, I think
putāre, to think
putāvī, I thought
putātum, thought
probō, I approve
probāre, to approve
probāvī, I approved
probātum, approved
vīvus, living
vīva, living
vīvum, living
mortuus, dead
mortua, dead
mortuum, dead
posterus, next
postera, next
posterum, next
postremus, last
postrema, last
postremum, last
extremus, outermost
extrema, outermost
extremum, outermost

Chapter 2

ceterus, the other
aequus, equal
beatus, happy, blessed

1st Conjugation (amō)		2nd Conjugation (videō)		NUMBER:
S	P	S	P	
amō	amāmus	videō	vidēmus	1st
amas	amātis	vides	vidētis	2nd
amat	amant	videt	vident	3rd

cetera, the other
aliena, strange

nullus, none
beatus, happy, blessed

aptum, apt, fitting
aequum, equal

pulchrum, beautiful
certa, certain

nulla, none
aequa, equal

ceterus, the other
aptus, apt, fitting

alienus, strange
beata, happy, blessed

alienum, strange
certum, certain

pulcher, beautiful
ceterum, the other

Chapter 3

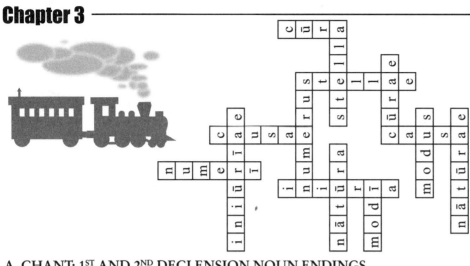

A. CHANT: 1ST AND 2ND DECLENSION NOUN ENDINGS

	1st Declension		2nd Declension (m)		2nd Declension (n)	
	S	P	S	P	S	P
Nominative:	-a	-ae	-us	-ī	-um	-a
Genitive:	-ae	-ārum	-ī	-ōrum	-ī	-ōrum
Dative:	-ae	-īs	-ō	-īs	-ō	-īs
Accusative:	-am	-ās	-um	-ōs	-um	-a
Ablative:	-ā	-īs	-ō	-īs	-ō	-īs

errāvī = I wandered

A	B	C	D	E	F	G	H	I	J	K	L	M	N	O	P	Q	R	S	T	U	V	W	X	Y	Z
18	22	3	16	17	4	10	9	24	21	1	11	15	23	20	5	8	13	19	26	7	14	2	12	6	25

ORŌ, I PRAY — 20 13 / 5 13 18 6
NĀTŪRA, NATURE, BIRTH — 23 / 18 26 / 13 18 / 23 18 26 7 13 17 / 22 24 13 26 9
ORNŌ, I EQUIP — 20 13 23 / 24 / 17 8 7 24 5
CAUSA, CAUSE — 16 18 7 19 18 / 16 18 7 19 17
PROBĀRE, TO APPROVE — 5 13 20 22 / 18 13 17 / 26 20 / 18 5 5 13 20 14 17
VĪVUS, LIVING — 14 / 14 7 19 / 11 24 14 14 24 23 10
MORTUUS, DEAD — 15 20 13 26 7 7 19 / 3 17 18 3
POSTERA, NEXT — 5 / 20 19 26 17 13 18 / 23 17 12 26
CŪRA, CARE — 16 / 13 18 / 16 18 13 17
EXTREMUM, OUTERMOST — 17 12 26 13 17 15 7 15 / 20 7 26 17 13 15 20 19 26
CERTUS, -CERTAIN — 16 17 13 26 7 19 / 16 17 13 26 18 24 23
STELLAE, STAR — 19 26 17 11 11 18 17 / 19 26 18 13
PULCHER, BEAUTIFUL — 5 7 11 16 9 17 13 / 22 17 18 7 26 24 4 7 11
ALIENUS, STRANGE — 18 11 24 17 23 7 19 / 19 26 13 18 23 10 17
NUMERĪ, NUMBER, MEASURE — 23 7 15 17 13 / 23 7 15 22 17 13 / 15 17 18 19 7 13 17

Chapter 4

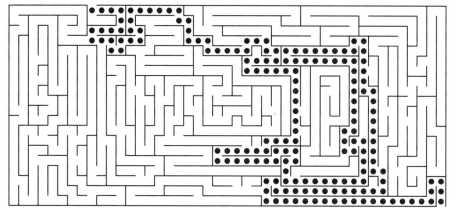

Robin Hood

agitō = to drive, stir up, agitate
vitium = fault
imperō = to order or command

	Present		Imperfect		Future	
	Singular	Plural	Singular	Plural	Singular	Plural
1st person	sum	sumus	eram	eramus	erō	erimus
2nd person	es	estis	eras	eratis	eris	eritis
3rd person	est	sunt	erat	erant	erit	erunt

Chapter 5

it's KING LATIN!

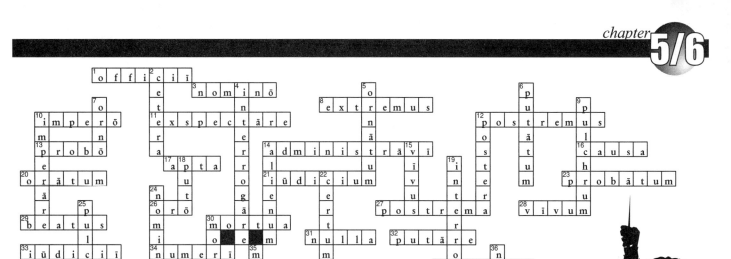

Chapter 6

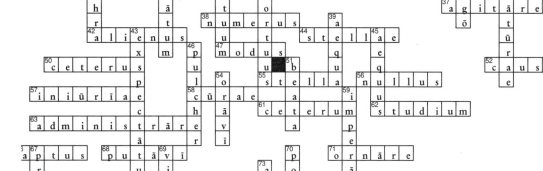

NUMBER	SINGULAR		
Gender	Masculine	Feminine	Neuter
Nominative	is	ea	id
Genitive	eius	eius	eius
Dative	eī	eī	eī
Accusative	eum	eam	id
Ablative	eō	eā	eō

WORDS NOT FOUND:
hōra, hour
lacrima, tear
iānua, door
eam, her (accusative case)

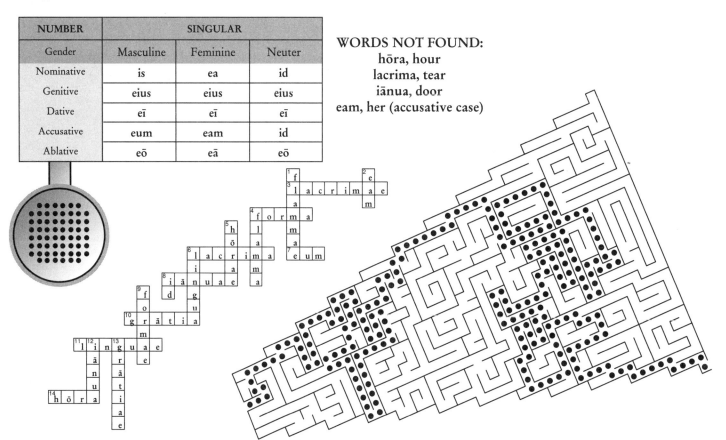

Chapter 6 cont.

Femina casam ornat.
A woman decorates a house.

Filia eius casam pulchram videt.
The daughter of her/Her daughter sees the pretty house.

"Casa pulchra est!" filia clamat.
"The house is pretty!" the daughter shouts.

Filius eius dicit quoque, "Ea pulchra est!"
The son of her/Her son also says, "It is pretty!"

Femina amublat ad eum et dicit, "Multas gratias ago tibi."
The woman walks to him and says, "Many thanks I give to you/Thank you very much."

Filia tristis (sad) est. Femina videt filiam et lacrimas eius.
The daughter is sad. The woman sees the daughter and her tears.

Femina ambulat ad eam et dicit, "Multas gratias ago etiam (also) tibi."
The woman walks to here and says, "Many thanks I give also to you."

Nunc (now) filia laetus est. Ea dicit, "Amo te mater!"
Now the daughter is happy. She says, "I love you mom!

Chapter 7

ŪLAN, OMNO
LŪNA, MOON
(11)

REOIAMM, YMMERO
MEMORIA, MEMORY
(10)

NŪALE, NMOO
LŪNAE, MOON

XAULŪRI, UYLXUR, EATXVNARCGAE
LUXŪRIA, LUXURY, EXTRAVAGANCE
(9)

EAGLĪT, UYETDP, NUTELTAENI
LEGATĪ, DEPUTY, LIEUTENANT
(8)

RMOAIEM, EMROYM
MEMORIA, MEMORY

TTAILEER, ETELTR
LITTERAE, LETTER
(2)

ERPAO, FRFTOE, RCEISSVE
OPERA, EFFORT, SERVICES
(3)

ĪLOUC, EEY
OCULĪ, EYE
(5)

ORPAEE, TFFOER, EREICSVS
OPERAE, EFFORT, SERVICES
(4)

ILTRETA, ERLTTE
LITTERA, LETTER
(6)

LSEAGTU, TEDPYU, ATUENTLENI
LEGATUS, DEPUTY, LIEUTENANT
(1)

RIALUXEŪ, XURUYL, EAEATNVRGCXA
LUXŪRIAE, LUXURY, EXTRAVAGANCE

UUOCSL, YEE
OCULUS, EYE

YEAh FOR LATIN!
1 2 3   4 5 6   7 8 9 10 11

NUMBER			PLURAL		
Gender	Masculine		Feminine		Neuter
Nominative: (SN, PN)	eī		eae		ea
Genitive: "of"	eōrum		eārum		eōrum
Dative: "to/for" (IO)	eīs		eīs		eīs
Accusative: (DO, OP)	eōs		eās		ea
Ablative: (OP)	eīs		eīs		eīs

Dear Great Great Aunt Loise,

I am writting you this letter, and hope that it finds you very happy. I wanted to offer you thanks for the wonderful dinner you offered my friends and I the other evening when the stars were out and the beautiful moon was quite large.

I enjoyed our talk around the table even though Alice secretly thought it was miserable. I really didn't know that at one point you were a sailor adventuring on the open sea with the wind in your hair. And the time you killed eight wolves with your bare hands. Is it really true that you jumped through a window and rode a wild horse while you were nearly blind? What a story! You caused me think when you told us about the dirty iron door that you had to open every day for school—and uphill both ways at that! it was your tale about climbing that tall mountain and your nearly freezing to death that surprised me the most. And I thought you just did needle point!

Love and kisses.

Chapter 8

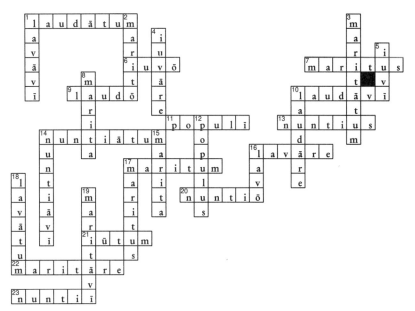

	Singular	Plural
Nominative (SN, PN)	ego	nōs
Genitive "of" (PNA)	meī	nostrum, nostrī
Dative "to/for" (IO)	mihi	nōbīs
Accusative (DO, OP)	mē	nōs
Ablative (OP)	mē	nōbīs

opera - effort, services
laudātum - to praise
maritō - to marry
lacrima, tear
iūdiciī, trial, legal investigation
causa, cause
aequum, equal

Chapter 9

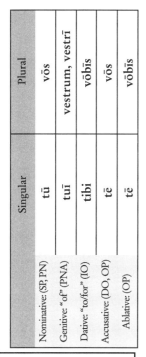

	Singular	Plural
Nominative: (SP, PN)	tū	vōs
Genitive: "of" (PNA)	tuī	vestrum, vestrī
Dative: "to/for" (IO)	tibi	vōbīs
Accusative: (DO, OP)	tē	vōs
Ablative: (OP)	tē	vōbīs

amovēre = move away
remus = oar
bellum = war, battle

sacculus = little bag
proelium = battle
adiuvō = help, aid

moveō = move
gladius = sword
avocō = call away

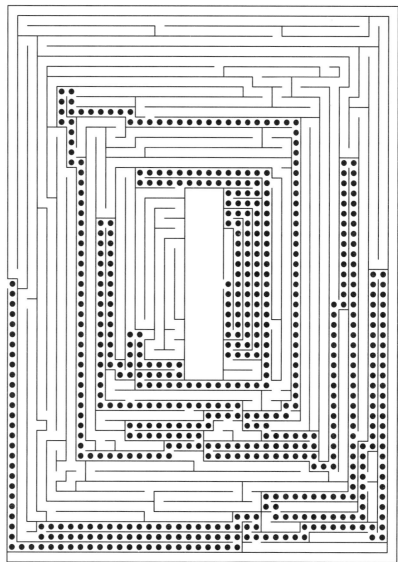

Chapter 10

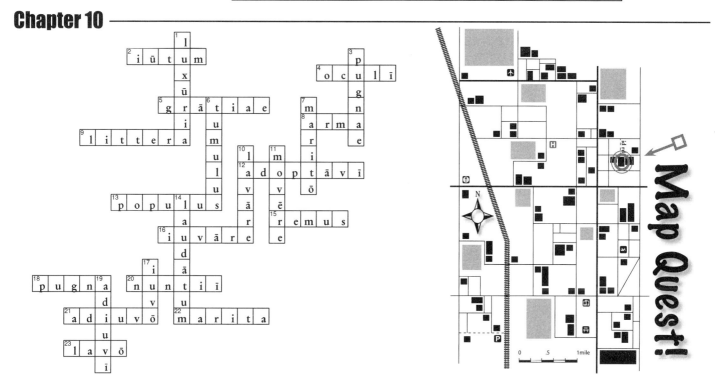

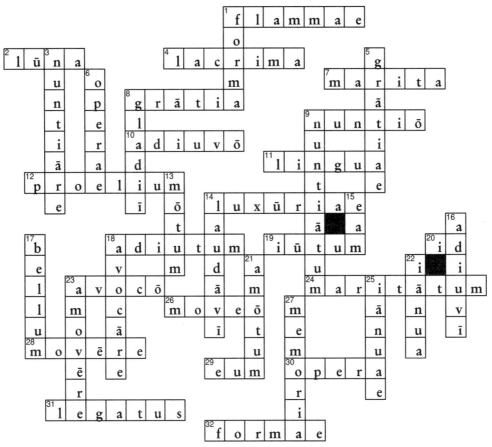

Chapter 11

	Present		Imperfect		Future	
	Singular	Plural	Singular	Plural	Singular	Plural
1st person	eō	īmus	ībam	ībāmus	ībō	ībimus
2nd person	is	ītis	ībās	ībātis	ībis	ībitis
3rd person	it	eunt	ībat	ībant	ībit	ībunt

PREPOSITION	MEANING	PREPOSITION	MEANING
ad	to, toward	ob	in front of
ante	before	per	through
apud	among, by, at, near	post	after
circā	around	praeter	past
contrā	against	prope	near
extrā	outside	propter	on account of
in + acc.	into	secundum	along
infrā	below	sub + acc.	up to
inter	between	super	over, above, beyond
intrā	within	suprā	over, above, on top of
iuxtā (juxta*)	near	trāns	across
		ultrā	beyond

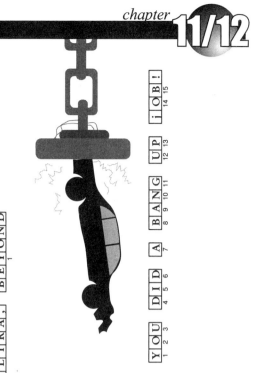

AD, TO, AROWDT
| AD, | TO, | TOWARD |
6

UAPD, NAMOG,YB, TA, ERAN
| APUD, | AMONG, | BY, | AT, | NEAR |
13 8

ÄCCRI, ONARDU
| CIRCÄ, | AROUND |
4

TONRÄC, AIGNATS
| CONTRÄ, | AGAINST |
5

NI + CAC, IONT
| IN | + | ACC., | INTO |
2

RÄNFI, BWOEL
| INFRÄ, | BELOW |
10

ÄRNT, IITHNW
| INTRÄ, | WITHIN |

BO, NI FNTOR OF
| OB, | IN | FRONT | OF |
14

PRE, OTHHRUG
| PER, | THROUGH |
11

ATEPRER, TAPS
| PRAETER, | PAST |
7

PPREORT, NO AONCUTC OF
| PROPTER, | ON | ACCOUNT | OF |
9 12

BSU + CAC., UP TO
| SUB | + | ACC., | UP | TO |
15 3

ÄRTLU, ENYOBD
| ULTRÄ, | BEYOND |
1

| YOU | DID | A | BANG | UP | ¡OB! |
1 2 3 / 4 5 6 / 7 / 8 9 10 11 / 12 13 / 14 15

Chapter 12

NUMBER:	PRESENT S	PRESENT P	IMPERFECT S	IMPERFECT P
1st	ferō	ferimus	ferēbam	ferēbāmus
2nd	fers	fertis	ferēbās	ferēbātis
3rd	fert	ferunt	ferēbat	ferēbant

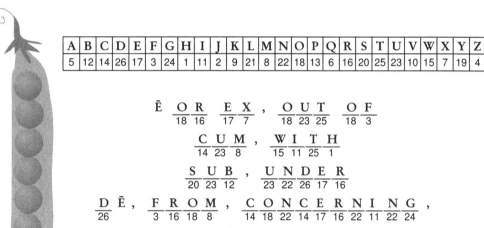

A	B	C	D	E	F	G	H	I	J	K	L	M	N	O	P	Q	R	S	T	U	V	W	X	Y	Z
5	12	14	26	17	3	24	1	11	2	9	21	8	22	18	13	6	16	20	25	23	10	15	7	19	4

Ē OR EX, OUT OF
18 16 17 7 18 23 25 18 3

CUM, WITH
14 23 8 15 11 25 1

SUB, UNDER
20 23 12 23 22 26 17 16

DĒ, FROM, CONCERNING,
26 3 16 18 8 14 18 22 14 17 16 22 11 22 24

ABOUT
5 12 18 23 25

TENUS, TO THE EXTENT
25 17 22 23 20 25 18 25 1 17 17 7 25 17 22 25

OF
18 3

IN, IN, ON
11 22 11 22 18 22

PRAE, IN FRONT OF
13 16 5 17 11 22 3 16 18 22 25 18 3

Ā OR AB, FROM, BY
18 16 5 12 3 16 18 8 12 19

PRŌ, BEFORE, ON BEHALF
13 16 12 17 3 18 16 17 18 22 12 17 1 5 21 3

OF
18 3

SINE, WITHOUT
20 11 22 17 15 11 25 1 18 23 25

CŌRAM, FACE-TO-FACE WITH
14 16 5 8 3 5 14 17 25 18 3 5 14 17 15 11 25 1

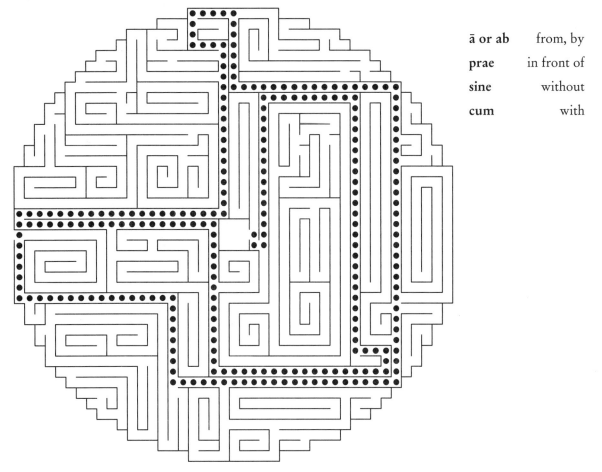

ā or ab	from, by
prae	in front of
sine	without
cum	with

Chapter 13

```
A Y C E I O A W N E U E L F W J B E F O R E Q Z V D T W I O
O M O B N V T R I B S D I R F M I K F Z R E T D D J W I N U
U W O T T E I H O T X J T O Y M S U V A Q L U L Q A P T F T
N N B N O R A V R U H J M M F A C E T O F A C E W I T H R S
E U D E G A R C V G N A C C O U N T O F A V O U T O F O O I
A Z V E F B N E A R U D L O B E T W E E N U P T O N I U N D
R T Y H R O Y E Y I W G W N A E B Y W R S V P C T O E T T E
D Y C K C V R A P O N R H C L D R O R U A C L C H X B Z O I
I U V O E E F E T Q N S H E O Q B E L O W S D O E H N W F D
K N S Z D B R S O N X D T R N A K C U V A J T T E Y Y D B K
O P F D V E O A O N E U C N G Q K U Q M O N D D X G O X N M
H U U R C Y M J F B B A B I L E J B W Y G D T T T L R U Z C
W J I V O O B K D T D E R N J H E H P U B K W A E M G N C U
I D Q N E I Y D M W E V H G O V E R A B O V E O N T O P O F
T D O M P D T K N M E R X A R A S H Y F J T H F T H K I D U
H M Q X P F M O Q V J N E B L A C R O S S Q Y X O T U Z S D
I Q I Q I T K R F N J L E O G F R F F H J A F M F P G E V D
N Y N J N K K I B N B X E U G T O T O W A R D W N J R B B W
V R O B Q I U Z F W S C M T H B O F B J V L E U J Q F E Z L
X V N J W H B P Q T M G D C A V Z I M H E E D D L F T J V D
```

ORSSMEPUT, LTAS
P O S T R E M U S ,   L A S T
16   22   7

ACETR, CETRIAN
C E R T A ,   C E R T A I N
10

NUMRĪE, MRBENU, ERMSEAU
N U M E R Ī ,   N U M B E R ,   M E A S U R E
                      19 9

MVIUN, IENW
V I N U M ,   W I N E
3   15 13

ŌRHAE, RUHO
H Ō R A E ,   H O U R
23 18 2

EERAMMO, OYMREM
M E M O R A E ,   M E M O R Y
5   24

MŌTAIR, TO AYMRR
M A R I T Ō ,   T O   M A R R Y
1

AĪVUDI, ELHP, DAI
A D I U V Ī ,   H E L P ,   A I D
12   8 14 21   4

USUNCMDE, AGOLN
S E C U N D U M ,   A L O N G
11 17

ISNE, HOTUTIW
S I N E ,   W I T H O U T
6   20

R E V I E W   T H E   R E V I E W
1 2 3 4 5 6   7 8 9   10 11 12 13 14 15
V O C A B U L A R Y !
12 16 17 18 19 20 21 22 23 24

Chapter 14

Latin cardinal numbers	English cardinal numbers
ūnus, ūna, ūnum	one
duo, duae, duo	two
trēs, tria	three
quattuor	four
quinque	five
sex	six
septem	seven
octō	eight
novem	nine
decem	ten

4	+	7	+	2	13
+		+		+	
1	+	8	+	6	15
+		+		+	
3	+	9	+	5	17
8		24		13	

6	-	1	-	8	-3
-		+		+	
9	-	7	-	5	-3
+		+		+	
2	-	4	+	3	1
-1		12		16	

ū	n	u	s	,		o	n	e	
n	o	v	e	m	,		n	i	n	e
	d	e	c	e	m	,		t	e	n
	ū	n	u	m	,		o	n	e
t	r	i	a	,		t	h	r	e	e
	d	u	a	e	,		t	w	o
t	r	ē	s	,		t	h	r	e	e
	d	u	o	,		t	w	o
q	u	i	n	q	u	e	,		f	i	v	e
s	e	p	t	e	m	,		s	e	v	e	n
	ū	n	a	,		o	n	e
	s	e	x	,		s	i	x
	o	c	t	ō	,		e	i	g	h	t
q	u	a	t	t	u	o	r	,		f	o	u	r

Chapter 15

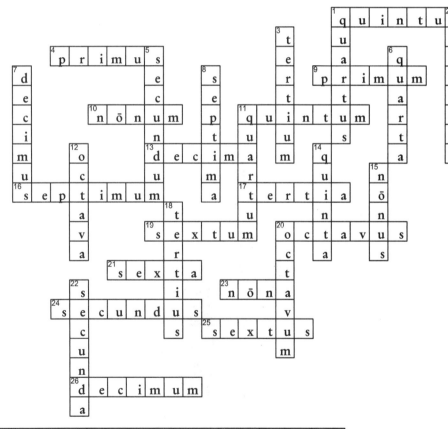

Latin	English
primus, a, um	first
secundus, a, um	second
tertius, a, um	third
quartus, a, um	fourth
quintus, a, um	fifth
sextus, a, um	sixth
septimus, a, um	seventh
octavus, a, um	eighth
nōnus, a, um	ninth
decimus, a, um	tenth

Gender	Masculine	Feminine	Neuter
Nominative	ūnus	ūna	ūnum
Genitive	ūnīus	ūnīus	ūnīus
Dative	ūnī	ūnī	ūnī
Accusative	ūnum	ūnam	ūnum
Ablative	ūnō	ūnā	ūnō

Chapter 16

	MASCULINE	FEMININE	NEUTER
Nominative	duo	duae	duo
Genitive	duōrum	duārum	duōrum
Dative	duōbus	duābus	duōbus
Accusative	duōs	duās	duo
Ablative	duōbus	duābus	duōbus

Joan of Arc - 1412
Sir Francis Bacon - 1561
Blaise Pascal - MDCXXIII
George Fredrick Handel -
MDCLXXXV
Wolfgang Amadeus Mozart - 1756
Davy Crockett - MDCCLXXXVI
Abraham Lincoln - 1809
Robert Louis Stevenson - MDCCCL
Madame Curie - MDCCCLXVII
Greta Garbo - MCMV

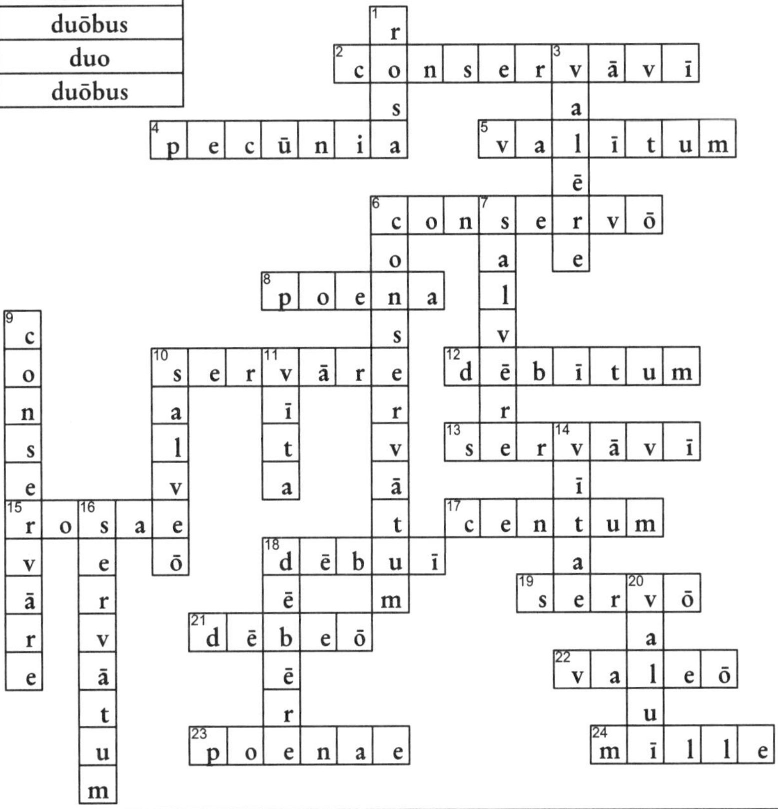

(Crossword puzzle with answers)

2 across: conservāvī
4 across: pecūnia
5 across: valītum
6 across: conservō
8 across: poena
10 across: servāre
12 across: dēbitum
13 across: servāvī
15 across: rosae
17 across: centum
18 across: dēbuī
19 across: servō
21 across: dēbeō
22 across: valeō
23 across: poenae
24 across: mīlle

Down: ros, ava, conservātum, consenser, salvavī, cōnsevāre, poenārum, alta, rītātā, debret, cī, a, serve, ēem, ēer, aum

Chapter 17

(Word search grid)

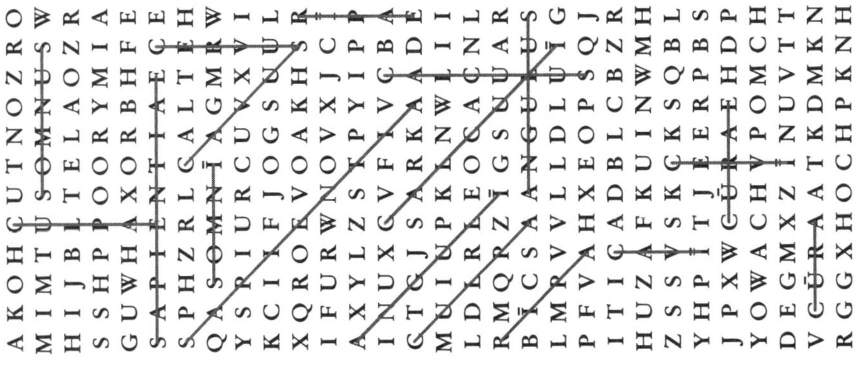

sapienta, wisdom
sapientae, wisdom
cüra, care
cürae, care
culpa, fault, blame, sin
culpae, fault, blame,
    sin
rïpa, river bank
rïpae, river bank
somnus, sleep
somnï, sleep
angulus, angle

angulï, angle
calculus, pebble
calculï, pebble
cavus, hole
cavï, hole
cervus, stag, deer
cervï, stag, deer

	Masculine and/or Feminine	Neuter
Nominative	trēs	tria
Genitive	trium	trium
Dative	tribus	tribus
Accusative	trēs	tria
Ablative	tribus	tribus

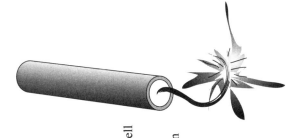

Across
1. against
3. hole
5. pebble
7. in, on
8. rose
9. sentence
11. be strong, be well
13. star
14. past
15. fault, blame, sin
16. life
17. to save
19. from, concern-
ing, about
21. eight
22. near

Down
1. stag, deer
2. to be well
4. after
5. care
6. tear
7. door
8. river bank
10. middle
12. hundred
13. wisdom
18. nine
20. out of

Chapter 18

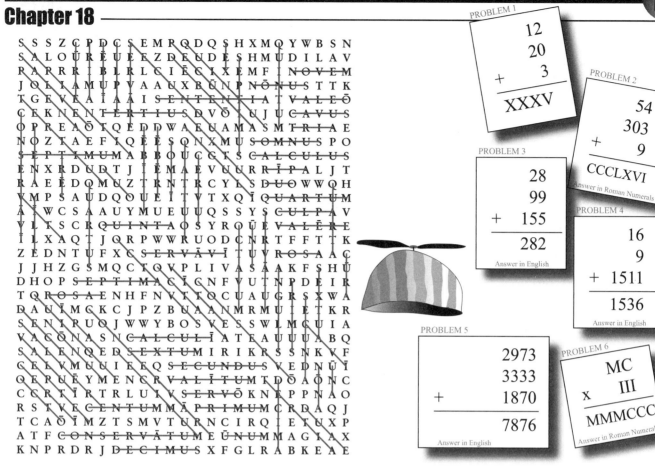

PROBLEM 1

$$\begin{array}{r} 12 \\ 20 \\ +3 \\ \hline XXXV \end{array}$$

PROBLEM 2

$$\begin{array}{r} 54 \\ 303 \\ +9 \\ \hline CCCLXVI \end{array}$$

Answer in Roman Numerals

PROBLEM 3

$$\begin{array}{r} 28 \\ 99 \\ +155 \\ \hline 282 \end{array}$$

Answer in English

PROBLEM 4

$$\begin{array}{r} 16 \\ 9 \\ +1511 \\ \hline 1536 \end{array}$$

Answer in English

PROBLEM 5

$$\begin{array}{r} 2973 \\ 3333 \\ +1870 \\ \hline 7876 \end{array}$$

Answer in English

PROBLEM 6

$$\begin{array}{r} MC \\ \timesIII \\ \hline MMMCCC \end{array}$$

Answer in Roman Numerals

Latin	English derivatives
ūnus, ūna, ūnum	one, unit, unity, union, united, unite
trēs, tria	three, triple, triplets, trio, tricycle, triad, trinity, triangle
quattuor	quarter, quartet, quart, quadruplets
sex	six, sextet, sextuplets
septem	September (originally it was the 7th month), septet, septuplets
decem	December (original 10th month), decade, decimate
primus, -a, -um	prime, primary, primal, primeval
secundus, -a, -um	second, secondary
quartus, -a, -um	quart, quarter
decimus, -a, -um	decimate
centum	century, centimeter, centipede, cent, centennial
mille	millennium, millennial, million
conservō	conservation, conserve, conservative
servō	serve, servant, servile, serf
dēbeō	debt, debit, indebted, indebt
valeō	valor, valiant, prevail
rosa, -ae	rose, rosy
cūra, -ae	care, cure, curator
glōria, -ae	glory, glorification, glorify
somnus, -ae	somnolent, insomnia, somnambulist (sleep-walker)
angulus, -ae	angle, angular
calculus, -ae	calculate, calculator, Calculus
cavus, -ī	cave, cavern, cavernous
silentium, -ī	silent

Chapter 19

	Singular	Plural
Nominative	-x	- ēs
Genitive	-is	-um
Dative	-ī	-ibus
Accusative	-em	- ēs
Ablative	-e	-ibus

sedeō, to sit
timeō, to fear, be afraid of
rex, king
respondī, to respond

soror, sister
principis, (c) leader, first one, prince
cīvitātis, (f) citizenship, state, commonwealth
respondī, to respond
rīdeō, to laugh, smile

Chapter 20

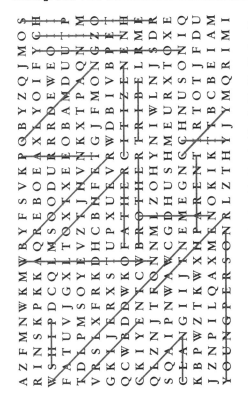

RTĀRFE	FRĀTER	
ĀRTISFR	FRĀTRIS	
ETMĀR	MĀTER	
ITMĀSR	MĀTRIS	
REĀPT	PĀTER	
TRĀSPI	PĀTRIS	
ĪISCV	CĪVIS	
VSCĪI	CĪVIS	
NRSĒPA	PARĒNS	
RATINPES	PARENTIS	
ĀNVIS	NĀVIS	
ĀINSV	NĀVIS	
IUEIVNS	IUVENIS	
EVIISNU	IUVENIS	
SNXEE	SENEX	
SISEN	SENIS	
RBUS	URBS	
SURBI	URBIS	
ĒNSG	GĒNS	
ENSTIG	GENTIS	

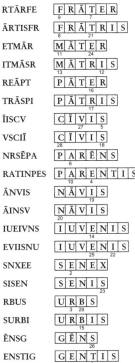

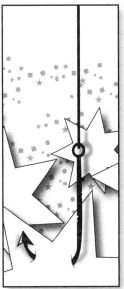

	Plural	Singular	
Nominative	-ēs	-x	
Genitive	-ium	-is	
Dative	-ibus	-ī	
Accusative	-ēs	-em	
Ablative	-ibus	-e	

Chapter 21

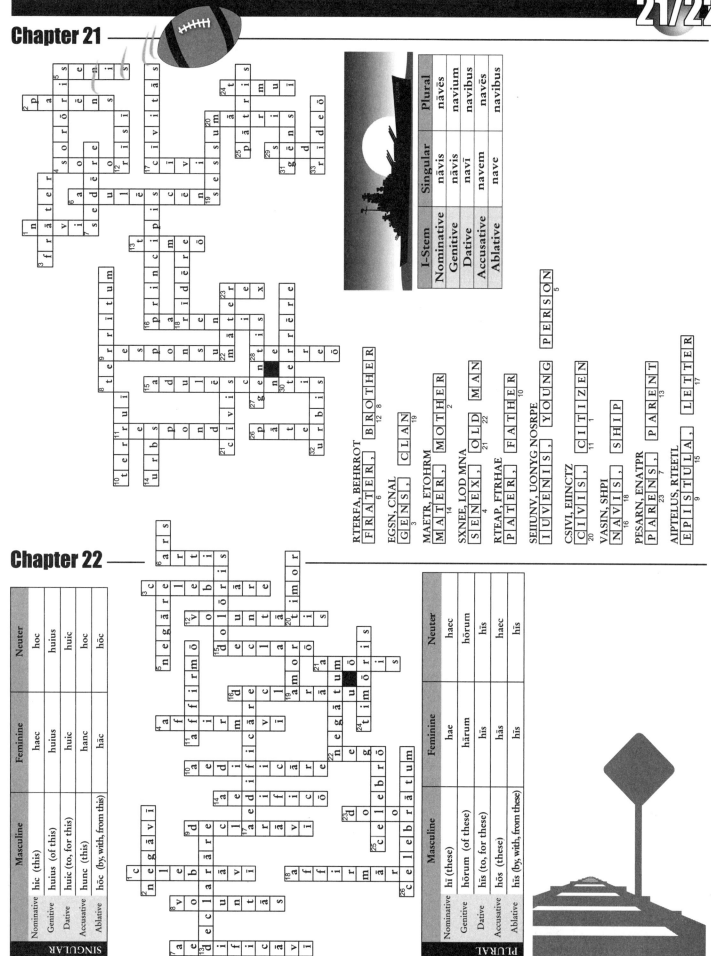

I-Stem	Singular	Plural
Nominative	nāvis	nāvēs
Genitive	nāvis	navium
Dative	navī	navibus
Accusative	navem	navēs
Ablative	nave	navibus

Chapter 22

	Masculine	Feminine	Neuter
Nominative	hic (this)	haec	hoc
Genitive	huius (of this)	huius	huius
Dative	huic (to, for this)	huic	huic
Accusative	hunc (this)	hanc	hoc
Ablative	hōc (by, with, from this)	hāc	hōc

SINGULAR

	Masculine	Feminine	Neuter
Nominative	hī (these)	hae	haec
Genitive	hōrum (of these)	hārum	hōrum
Dative	hīs (to, for these)	hīs	hīs
Accusative	hōs (these)	hās	haec
Ablative	hīs (by, with, from these)	hīs	hīs

PLURAL

Chapter 23

	CASE	MASCULINE	FEMININE	NEUTER
SINGULAR	Nom.	ille (that)	illa	illud
	Gen.	illius (of that)	illius	illius
	Dat.	illī (to, for that)	illī	illī
	Acc.	illum (that)	illam	illud
	Abl.	illō (by, with, from that)	illā	illō
PLURAL	Nom.	illī (those)	illae	illa
	Gen.	illōrum (of those)	illārum	illōrum
	Dat.	illīs (to, for those)	illīs	illīs
	Acc.	illōs (those)	illās	illa
	Abl.	illīs (by, with, from those)	illīs	illīs

Plur. Dat. Neut. illīs

mortuum, dead

uxor, (f) wife
noctis, (f) night
montis, (m, i) mountain

Chapter 24

iurāre, to take an oath
conservō, to keep, preserve

iūdicis, (m) judge
iurāre, to take an oath

damnāre, to condemn, punish
lex, (f) law, contract

iurāre, to take an oath
volātum, to fly

conservō, to keep, preserve
lēgis, (f) law, contract

volātum, to fly
auctor, (m) ancestor, originator, supporter

peccō, to sin, make a mistake
conservō, to keep, preserve

potestās, (f) power
iurātum, to take an oath

auctōritātis, (f) influence, authority
potestās, (f) power

damnō, to condemn, punish
volātum, to fly

iurō, to take an oath
iūdicis, (m) judge

	Case	Masculine	Feminine	Neuter
Singular	Nom.	iste (that)	ista	istud
	Gen.	istius (of that)	istius	istius
	Dat.	istī (to, for that)	istī	istī
	Acc.	istum (that)	istam	istud
	Abl.	istō (by, with, from that)	istā	istō
Plural	Nom.	istī (those)	istae	ista
	Gen.	istōrum (of those)	istārum	istōrum
	Dat.	istīs (to, for those)	istīs	istīs
	Acc.	istōs (those)	istās	ista
	Abl.	istīs (by, with, from those)	istīs	istīs

A	B	C	D	E	F	G	H	I	J	K	L	M	N	O	P	Q	R	S	T	U	V	W	X	Y	Z
8	12	18	15	11	26	19	14	3	20	5	7	1	22	16	25	21	17	6	9	4	2	23	13	24	10

VOLŌ, TO FLY
VOLĀTUM, TO FLY
PECCŌ, TO SIN — MAKE A MISTAKE
PECCĀVĪ, TO SIN — MAKE A MISTAKE
IURŌ, TO TAKE AN OATH
DAMNŌ, TO CONDEMN, PUNISH
CONCILIĀRE, TO BRING TOGETHER, UNITE
CONSERVŌ, TO KEEP, PRESERVE
IŪDEX, (M) JUDGE
POTESTĀTIS, (F) POWER
AUCTŌRITAS, (F) INFLUENCE, AUTHORITY
AUCTŌR, (M) ANCESTOR, ORIGINATOR, SUPPORTER
LEX, (F) LAW, CONTRACT
LĒGIS, (F) LAW, CONTRACT
AUCTŌRIS, (M)

Chapter 25

Pattern A has a simple form
It's made with a Verb and a Subject Noun
SN-V! SN-V!
Pattern A has a simple form!

Pattern B is a pattern of "B"eing
Two Nouns surround a small LV
SN-LV-PRN! SN-LV-PRN!
Pattern "B" is pattern of "B"eing!

Pattern C links a Noun to an Adjective
See the difference now—are you positive?
SN-LV-PA! SN-LV-PA!

Pattern D has an Action Verb
And one Direct Object—have you heard?
SN-Vt-DO! SN-Vt-DO!

Across
4. (m) horseman, knight, equestrian
9. (f) death
10. (m) blood
12. (m) robber, mercenary
14. (f) age
15. (m) talk, conversation, discourse
17. (c) stranger, foreigner, enemy (of one's country)
18. (f) speech, message

Down
1. (m) blood
2. (m) robber, mercenary
3. (c) stranger, foreigner, enemy (of one's country)
4. (m) horseman, knight, equestrian
5. (m) talk, conversation, discourse
6. (f) health
7. (f) speech, message
8. (c) soldier
9. (c) soldier
11. (f) age
13. (f) health
16. (f) death

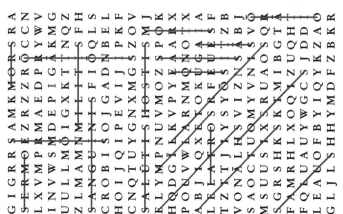

GridWork

MAGIC WORD:
ōrātiōnis = (f) speech, message

Chapter 26

A D X L B D C U D E S A Y L M O D O L Ō R I S U V
V F E U O F E X E Q B A E V N I S Q L A B Ō R I S
S O F C I R L O C U A T L D E C L A R Ā T U M C K
M Q X L X E R L E Q I Ū I N E I L Ā N W D C X
W I L S R A B A T D P L M I F E U I U I T O E A
C S L I Y M P S R N E G Ō I E X I S I L L E
L E J E S A Z Ā Ō S F A R S L R S C Ā L S L O E D
U V L T S F T V A A E D I F I C Ā V Ī A R B I
X I S E W F U B U I C V N O X J W S M R Ī B W R F
Y C Q J B M U E M Ā A Q V E S T I S Y E O C Ā
A T L A T R Ō N I S R R V L D E C L A R Ā R E V C
E O I M M Ā O W Q E T M E U C L A B O R N I Ō
R S S Q A Q R B L Q L O S N E D Y L N S O S D
Ā N V K R R U N E Y U S A Ū N T T E L X X C C M
T D E N S E T J S V E F F W C T I Ā E N O C T I
I E S E R M O I Q Q S A F U E L I S T B T W J P
S O T L A T R O S C A R X D X S S G I R I S H
I H T I M O R I Z T R O U X Ō R I S S Ō S Q
Q C S N E G Ā R E A K M R M B S V L D O G K
Ō R Ā T I Ō N I S N B S Ō G Q Q G E E A B T P T
C P S F M Y A F F I R M Ā V Ī R N V R S B L P
N H S A V O L U N T Ā S A N G U I S I M T O W S R
Q L W R N E G Ā T U M R I V I C T O R C Q I R O
W Q A G V C A G D B O A Q D W R V L O W T N S S
P R E T K U U W M K N W E V B W J Q R F Y Q K Y
Z U T I P U N I H Y T A M Ō R I S M L O V E R S G
M X A N N X Q Q N Y V Ō C I S A D E N S C X L O
H O S T I S X M S I S T C U C W J M S R M V R W S
X R X R O Z Q J G Y S D E N T I S V Q X T N V M K
Z K E N K E B L M X U A F B Q V B Z J R G E U U T

	CASE	MASCULINE	FEMININE	NEUTER
SINGULAR	Nom.	hic (this)	haec	hoc
	Gen.	huius (of this)	huius	huius
	Dat.	huic (to, for this)	huic	huic
	Acc.	hunc (this)	hanc	hoc
	Abl.	hōc (by, with, from this)	hāc	hōc
PLURAL	Nom.	hī (these)	hae	haec
	Gen.	hōrum (of these)	hārum	hōrum
	Dat.	hīs (to, for these)	hīs	hīs
	Acc.	hōs (these)	hās	haec
	Abl.	hīs (by, with, from these)	hīs	hīs

	CASE	MASCULINE	FEMININE	NEUTER
SINGULAR	Nom.	ille (that)	illa	ilud
	Gen.	illīus (of that)	illīus	illīus
	Dat.	illī (to, for that)	illī	illī
	Acc.	illum (that)	illam	illud
	Abl.	illō (by, with, from that)	illā	illō
PLURAL	Nom.	illī (those)	illae	illa
	Gen.	illōrum (of those)	illārum	illōrum
	Dat.	illīs (to, for those)	illīs	illīs
	Acc.	illōs (those)	illās	illa
	Abl.	illīs (by, with, from those)	illīs	illīs

ENGŌ, TO ENDY
NEGŌ, TO DENY
25 11

FIIEAŌDC, OT DUBLL, TREEC EISABTLHS
AEDIFICŌ, TO BUILD, ERECT ESTABLIISH
26 24 3

CDLAŌER, OT ADEERCL
DECLARŌ, TO DECLARE
21 16 23

RSA, (F) TRA, KSLLI
ARS, (F) ART, SKILL
27 10

LCISŪ, (F) LHGIT
LŪCIS, (F) LIIGHT
12 14

XVO, (F) COEVI
VOX, (F) VOICE
20 2

RPEÁCCE, TO NIS, KEAM A ESTIKAM
PECCĀRE, TO SIN, MAKE A MIISTAKE
4 19

MDŌAN, OT MDONNCE, NHSPUI
DAMNŌ, TO CONDEMN, PUNIISH
18 5

VCVNERĪOSĀ, OT KEPE, ERSEVEPR
CONSERVĀVĪ, TO KEEP, PRESERVE
6 9

OITĀPSTTSE, (F) PEORW
POTESTĀTIS, (F) POWER
9

XEL, (F) LWA, TCCNROAT
LEX, (F) LAW, CONTRACT
8 17

EĪLSM, (C) ORSLDIE
MĪLES, (C) SOLDIER
7

SULSA, (F) LEHHAT
SALŪS, (F) HEALTH
13 22

AITSÁET, (F) AEG
AETĀTIIS, (F) AGE
15

YOU'RE NEARIING THE END OF THE BOOK!
1 2 3 4 5 6 7 8 9 10 11 12 13 14 15 16 17 18 19 20 21 22 23

Chapter 27

Crossword answers (Chapter 27):

1. cecidī
2. dūxī
3. dūcō
4. cadere
5. crēdidī
6. scrībere
7. cāsum
8. credere
9. auris
10. fīnis
11. avis
12. fīnis
13. avis
14. cadō
15. cursum
16. hominis
17. scriptum

	SINGULAR	PLURAL
1st person	dūcō	dūcimus
2nd person	dūcis	dūcitis
3rd person	dūcit	dūcunt

Chapter 28

Scrambled	Answer
RSPA	P A R S (4)
NDNAIIISTGŪM	M A G N I T Ū D I N I S (15)
SPIED	P E D I S (9)(1)
NISUDITLŪMIT	M U L T I T Ū D I N I S (24)(21)
NÊSM	M Ē N S (23)
ÕIATR	R A T I Ō (3)(22)
MŌAGI	I M A G Ō (6)(27)
ETSINM	M E N T I S (2)
SSCIIP	P I S C I S (25)(11)
MIŪLTTUDŌ	M U L T I T Ū D Ō (5)
RISOB	O R B I S (14)(10)
RNAIITSO	R A T I O N I S (7)(18)
BSIRO	O R B I S (20)(12)
SITRPA	P A R T I S (26)(8)
NIIMIGAS	I M A G I N I S (10)
SPĒ	P Ē S (13)
CPSSII	P I S C I S (19)
AŪNGTŌIDM	M A G N I T Ū D Ō (17)

Cryptogram:

I hEAR ThAT ThERE IS
1 2 3 4 5 6 7 8 9 10 9 11 12

POTATOES ON ThE NExT PAGE.
13 14 15 16 17 18 9 19 20 21 22 2 23 2 24 25 26 27 2

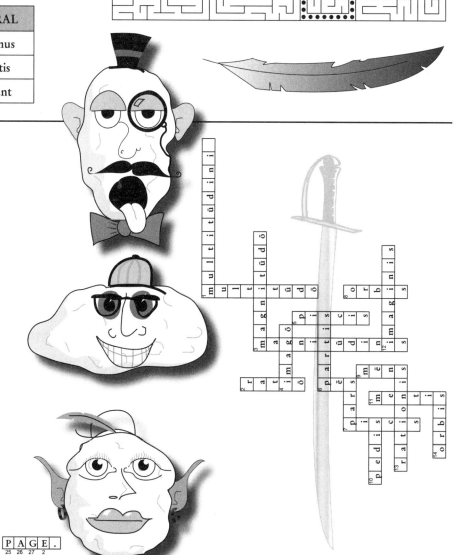

Chapter 29

	SING.	PLUR.
Nom.	-x	-a
Gen.	-is	-um
Dat.	-i	-ibus
Acc.	-x	-a
Abl.	-e	-ibus

	SING.	PLUR.
Nom.	-x	-a
Gen.	-is	-um
Dat.	-i	-ibus
Acc.	-x	-a
Abl.	-e	-ibus

Chapter 30

Across
1. (n, i) sea
3. (m) companion
5. (m) companion
9. command, order, power
10. footprint, trace, track
12. (n) journey, road
13. footprint, trace, track
16. (n) crime
17. command, order, power
19. (n) journey, road
21. business, occupation
22. (m) leader, ruler, commander

Down
2. (n, i) animal
4. (n) a work, a labor
6. (n, i) sea
7. (n, i) animal
8. business, occupation
11. (n) crime
14. (m) leader, ruler, commander
15. (n) a work, a labor
18. power, rule, realm
20. power, rule, realm

		PLURAL		
		-ia	-ium	-ibus
		-ia	-ibus	

	SINGULAR			
Nominative	-x			
Genitive	-is			
Dative	-ī			
Accusative	-x			
Ablative	-ī			

Cryptogram answers: MARE, OPUS, MARIS, SCELUS, ITINERIS, IMPERIUM, OPĒRIS, ITER, NEGŌTIĪ, VESTIGIUM, DUX, IMPERIĪ, NEGŌTIUM, VESTIGIĪ, REGNUM, REGNĪ, COMES, ANIMAL, DUCIS

Chapter 31

```
D O U Y T R V S F O S Q C O O X T J Z F
U P I S C I S I C F Z C R A I P F I L
C S V Y Z Y J B C R N C E B D Y L P V N
E U L A O Q H Y T I M E L I O U A H
R R C S U R G E R E U R A C U S M R O S
E G I U N E G O T I I M C I S E T M P
O O K Q R R G L I T U S Q U N D N
S P I M F R O C U R R E R E M I S N D
X O M I A C I S M D V L X N S M T Y
J N P I U P S U U I W O I U O U S S
E E T K E E K L I X X D U C T U M D L
M R R E J D C N T V I V E R E O R I S O
A E R T N H D A Z A I C Z F D I T
G S I F R D O G T U I U X L C E I T Z
S E Y K I M A U S R C R P A N K C I
N S C U L W E W D L J K T I P T I O N
I V C E V A N Q O A V I S U S N E S E
S B I R I T O L D G Q T G M I O R R D
W K N V I E M U L T I T U D I N I S O
C U R R O B R H S A X C O R P O R I S S
O R B I S A O I U N R A T I O D R G A D
X V V H C J X M S I V R N H T V C N B U
G F Q O R R I M U M Z U E Z U R W I U C
R E G N I T E M D A T M V G P K O S R O
B L N V N H H D E L T P V S N S F V R G
S C R I B E R E E N D I X I O U C C R O
P I X E Y W Q H D R S P E S D N M Q J U
V F V E S T I G I I E J X I P W S F X D
O P E R I S Q Q Q C R I M E N F I N I S
D C C C P F H V O J K J X X C F N P L G
```

ROUTE 66

2. imperium, command, order, power
5. pars, (f) part, portion
6. homō, (m) man, human being
1. pōnō, to put, place
8. scrībere, to write, engrave
3. currō, to run, hasten
7. vestigiī, footprint, trace, track
4. imagō, (f) image

1. opēris, (n) a work, a labor
4. comes, (m) companion
2. lītus, (n) shore, beach
3. surrēctum, to rise, get up
6. hominis, (m) man, human being
8. currere, to run, hasten
7. avis, (f,i) bird
5. piscis, (m,i) fish

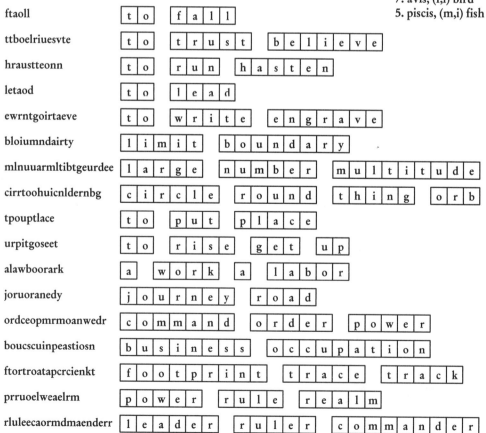

scramble	answer
ftaoll	to fall
ttboelriuesvte	to trust believe
hraustteonn	to run hasten
letaod	to lead
ewrntgoirtaeve	to write engrave
bloiumndairty	limit boundary
mlnuuarmltibtgeurdee	large number multitude
cirrtoohuicnldernbg	circle round thing orb
tpouptlace	to put place
urpitgoseet	to rise get up
alawboorark	a work a labor
joruoranedy	journey road
ordceopmrmoanwedr	command order power
boucscuinpeastiosn	business occupation
ftortroatapcrcienkt	footprint trace track
prruoelweaelrm	power rule realm
rluleecaormdmaenderr	leader ruler commander

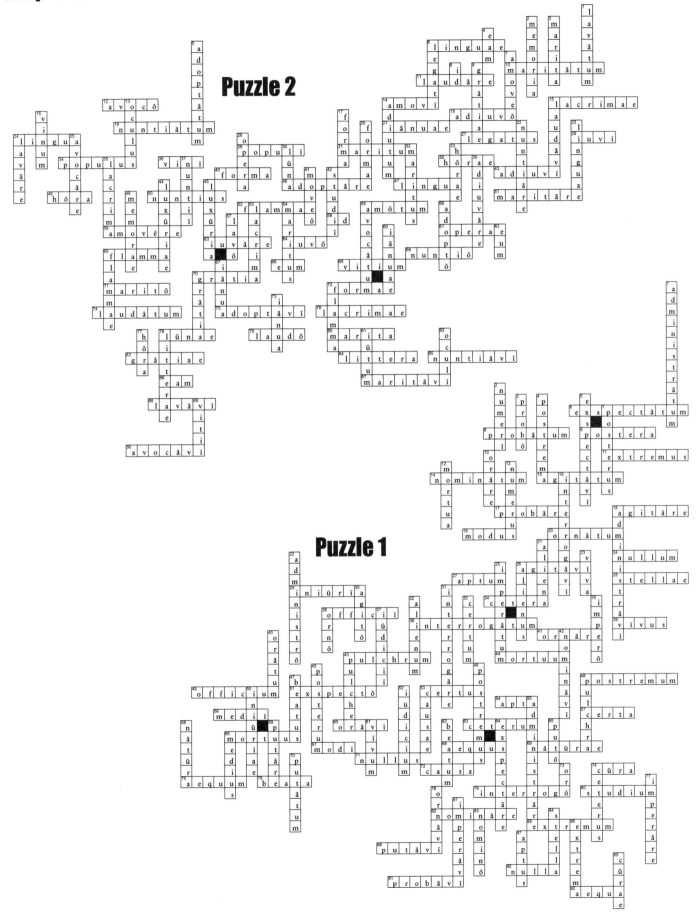

Puzzle 2

Puzzle 1

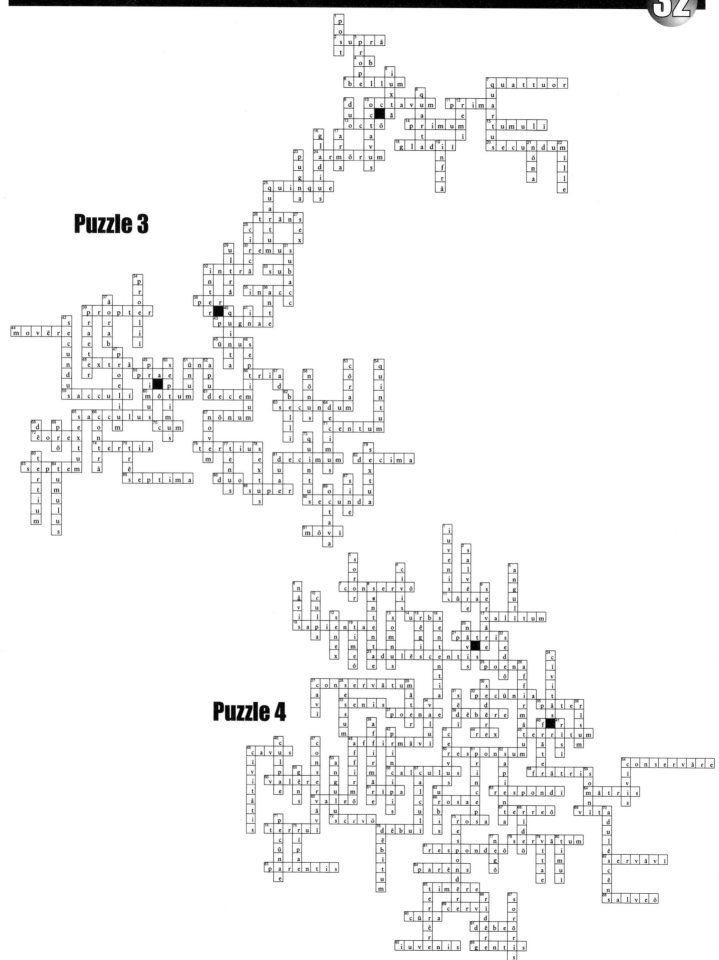

Puzzle 3

Puzzle 4

Puzzle 5

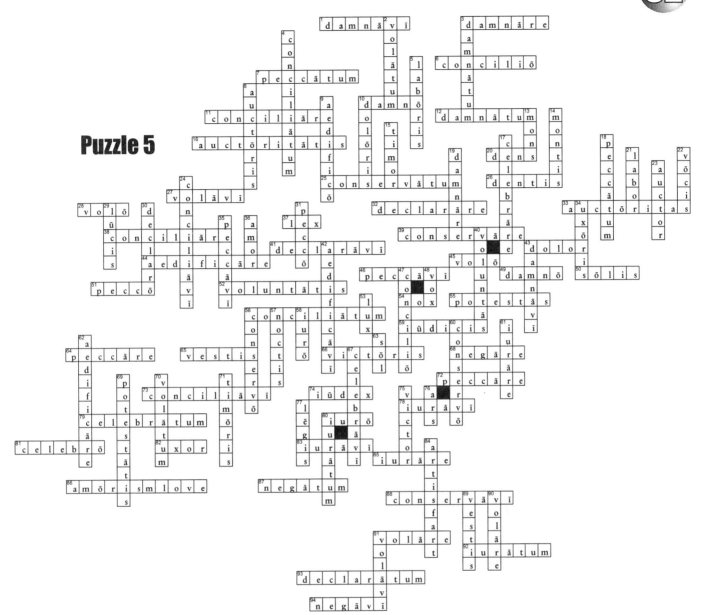

whopper crossword puzzle!

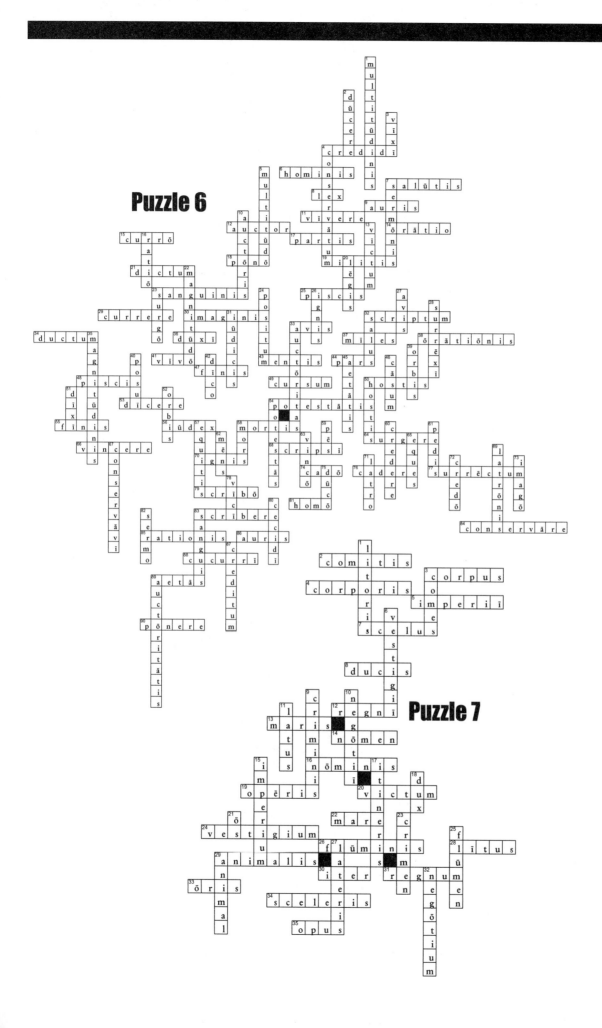

Puzzle 6

Puzzle 7

Look. Look Again!

4 games in 1

For use with the
Latin For Children, Primer B
vocabulary list.

INSTRUCTIONS:

Cut out all the black-colored Latin/English tiles.

NOTE: 1 matched set (Latin & English translation) = 1 point

GAME ONE: STANDARD _____
GAME PLAY: From 2 to 10 players

Select only the cards that you have learned so far.
Shuffle the deck (don't include dove or snake).

Spread out the cards (face down) across a table top or playing floor.

Game play begins with the player to the left of the dealer.

The player can flip any two cards (in place) of his/her choice. Make sure that all players get a chance to see the content of each card. If what was turned over matches (Latin and its correct English translation), AND the player recognizes the match, they may then remove that match and place those cards in front of themselves.

If a match occurs, the player may continue flipping sets of cards until no match is found.

If no match is found, all unmatched cards are flipped back over. Play continues with the next player.

Try your best to remember where previously revealed unmatched content is so that when the match is found you may return to it!

Person with the most matches wins!

GAME TWO: SHARK PIT _____
GAME PLAY: From 2 to 10 players

Shuffle (don't include dove or snake). Spread out the deck.

When the dealer says, "Go." everyone flips two cards at the same time.

The first person to spy any match on the table can grab it.

When all the matches have been found, the dealer says, "Go." again. Each individual will flip two more cards.

The first person to spy any matches can grab them.

The player with the most matches wins!

GAME THREE: MARKETPLACE
GAME PLAY: From 2 to 10 players

Shuffle (include dove & snake).

Deal out all the cards amongst all the players.

Each player may hold/look at the first 6 cards (but not more).

Players can immediately remove any matches in their hand and replenish their hand with cards from their deck.

The dealer declares that; "The market is open."

Cards can be swapped from one player to another:

> Cards swapped must be either all Latin cards or all English cards. No intermixing. The **only exception** is the dove and snake card. They can be included into any deal.
>
> Players swapping must exchange an equal number of cards.
>
> As the game continues, players should pull out their correct matches and replenish their hands (max 6 cards).
>
> EXAMPLE: One player may pull 4 English cards from his hand (without showing anyone the contents) and cry out "4 English, 4 English!" Another player may fulfill the exchange by swapping 4 English cards of their own.

The dove card gives you 2 extra points.

If you are holding the snake card when the hand/game ends you lose 5 points.

The first player with matches, who cries, "Retro Specto!" wins that hand. The first player to 25 points wins the game.

GAME FOUR: SOLITAIRE _____
GAME PLAY: For 1 player

Shuffle (include dove & snake). Spread out the deck face down.

Flip 5 cards in place. Pull out any/all matches.

Turn over remaining cards face down.

Flip 5 more cards. Pull any/all matches. *Can you match the entire deck without finding the animal cards more than 3 times total (1 time for each animal + one "oops")?*

ADDITIONAL IDEAS:

- For added durability, have the cards individually laminated (your local office supply store will likely offer lamination services).

- We encourage you to cut out the tiles by hand (a paper cutter works well, but cut one page at a time) since each page may not line up exactly with the next page.

- Change the end-game target points for a faster or longer game.

- Modify the rules to work best with your set of students.

orō, orāre, orāvī, orātum	ornō, ornāre, ornāvī, ornātum	putō, putāre, putāvī, putātum
probō, probāre, probāvī, probātum	vīvus, -a, -um	mortuus, -a, -um
posterus, -a, -um	postremus, -a, -um	certus, -a, -um
cēterus, -a, -um	pulcher, pulchra, pulchrum	aliēnus, -a, -um
aequus, -a, -um	causa, -ae	cūra, -ae

I conquer	river	mouth, face
body	crime, accusation	a name
sea	crime	animal
a work, a labor	journey, road	town
business, occupation	power, rule, realm	companion, friend

iniūria, -ae (injūria, -ae)	nātūra, -ae	stella, -ae
medius, -ī	modus, -ī	interrogō, interrogāre, interrogāvī, interrogātum
agitō, agitāre, agitāvī, agitātum	imperō, imperāre, imperāvī, imperātum	administrō, administrāre, administrāvī, administrātum
nominō, nomināre, nomināvī, nominātum	iudicium, -ī (judicium, -ī)	officium, -ī
studium, -ī	vīnum, -ī	vitium, -ī

robber, mercenary	horseman, knight, equestrian	death
blood	age	to trust, believe
to lead	bird	man, human being
image	greatness	large number, multitude
foot	to speak	I live

eum	eam	flamma, -ae
fōrma, -ae	grātia, -ae	hōra, -ae
iānua, -ae (jānua, -ae)	lacrima, -ae	littera, -ae
lūna, -ae	luxūria, -ae	memoria, -ae
opera, -ae	lēgātus, -ī	numerus, -ī

to strengthen, assert, affirm	to build, erect establish	to declare
love	wife	light
night	voice	the sun
to fly	to sin, make a mistake	to bring together, unite
judge	influence, authority	speech, message

iuvō, iuvāre, iūvī, iūtum	laudō, laudāre, laudāvī, laudātum	lavō, lavāre, lavāvī, lavātum
nuntiō, nuntiāre, nuntiāvī, nuntiātum	maritō, maritāre, maritāvī, maritātum	maritus/marita
maritus, -a, -um	nūntius, ī	adiuvō, adiuvāre, adiūvī, adiūtum
adoptō, adoptāre, adoptāvī, adoptātum	amoveō, amovēre, amovī, amōtum	avocō, avocāre, avocāvī, avocātum
rēmus, -ī	sacculus, -ī	tumulus, -ī

RETRO Specto™

RETRO Specto™

RETRO Specto™

RETRO Specto™

RETRO Specto™

RETRO Specto™

RETRO Specto™

RETRO Specto™

RETRO Specto™

RETRO Specto™

RETRO Specto™

RETRO Specto™

RETRO Specto™

RETRO Specto™

RETRO Specto™

sleep	pebble	hole
to respond	to laugh, smile	to terrify, frighten
to fear, be afraid of	leader, first one, prince	sister
brother	mother	father
parent	ship	old man

RETRO Specto™

RETRO Specto™

RETRO Specto™

RETRO Specto™

RETRO Specto™

RETRO Specto™

RETRO Specto™

RETRO Specto™

RETRO Specto™

RETRO Specto™

RETRO Specto™

RETRO Specto™

RETRO Specto™

RETRO Specto™

RETRO Specto™

affirmō, affirmāre, affirmāvī, affirmātum (also spelled "adfirmō")	aedificō, aedificāre, aedificāvī, aedificātum	declarō, declarāre, declarāvī, declarātum
amor, amōris (m)	uxor, uxōris (f)	lux, lūcis (f)
nox, noctis (f, i)	vox, vōcis (f)	sōl, sōlis (m)
volō, volāre, volāvī, volātum	peccō, peccāre, peccāvī, peccātum	conciliō, conciliāre, conciliāvī, conciliātum
iūdex, iūdicis (m) (iūdex, iūdicis [m])	auctōritas, auctōritātis (f)	ōrātio, ōrātiōnis (f)

to help	to praise	to wash
to announce	to marry	husband/ wife
married	messenger	help, aid
select, adopt	move away	call away
oar	little bag	hill, mound

RetroSpecto™

RetroSpecto™
RetroSpecto™
RetroSpecto™
RetroSpecto™
RetroSpecto™
RetroSpecto™
RetroSpecto™
RetroSpecto™
RetroSpecto™
RetroSpecto™
RetroSpecto™
RetroSpecto™
RetroSpecto™
RetroSpecto™

vincō, vincere, vīcī, victum	flūmen, flūminis (n)	ōs, ōris (n)
corpus, corporis (n)	crīmen, crīminis (n)	nōmen, nōmenis (n)
mare, maris (n), (i)	scelus, sceleris (n)	animal, animalis (n), (i)
opus, operis (n)	iter, itineris, (n)	oppidum, -ī (n)
negōtium, -ī (n)	regnum, -ī (n)	comes, comitis (m)

equal	cause	care
the other	beautiful	strange
next	last	certain
dead	living	I approve, to approve, I approved, approved
I think, to think, I thought, thought	I equip, to equip, I equipped, equipped	I pray, to pray, I prayed, prayed

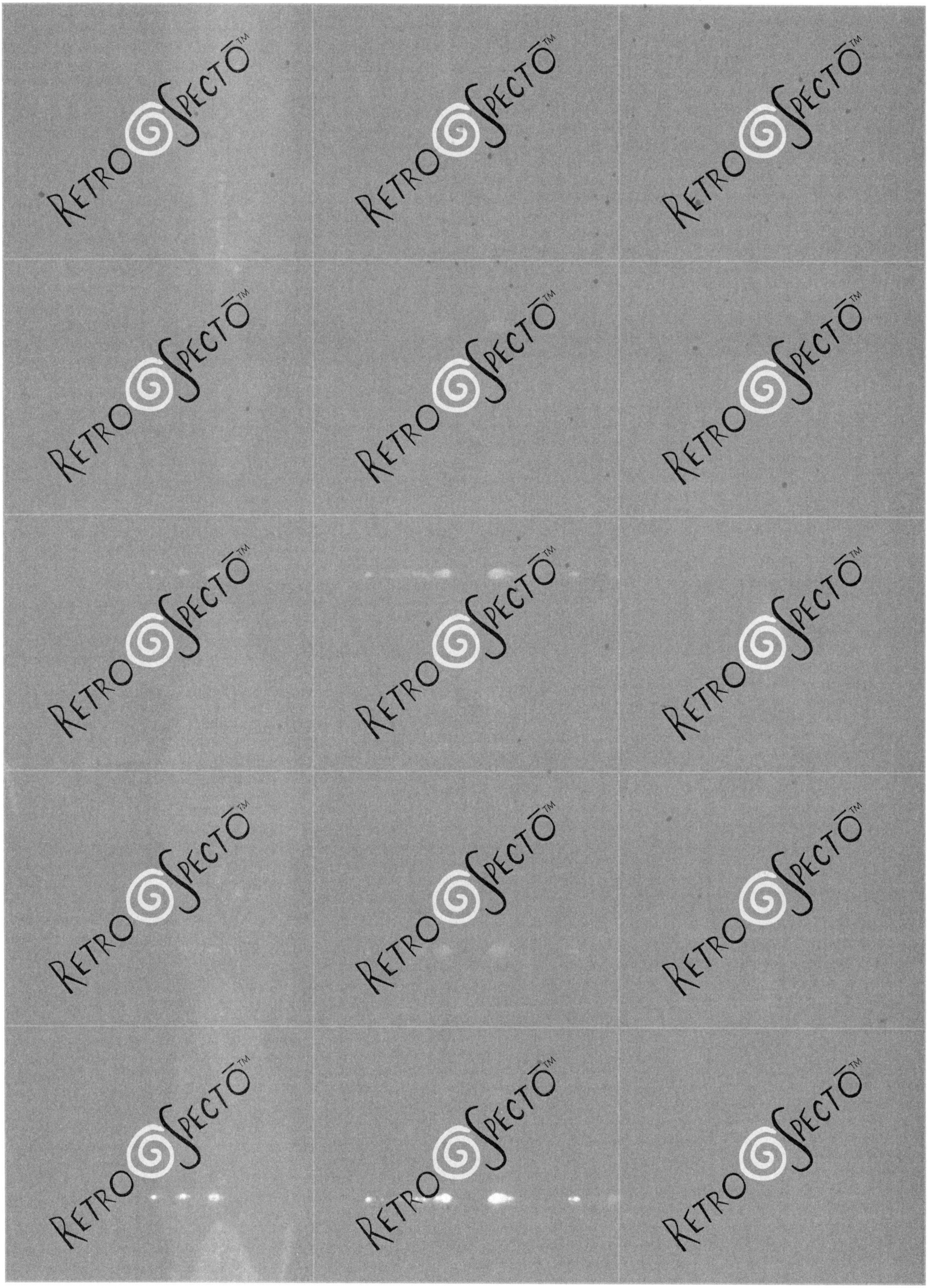

gladius, -ī	bellum, -ī	arma, -ōrum (plural only)
ūnus, ūna, ūnum	duo, duae, duo	trēs, tria
quattuor	quīnque	septem
novem	decem	prīmus, -a, -um
tertius, -a, -um	quartus, -a, -um	quīntus, -a, -um

RETRO SPECTŌ™

RETRO SPECTŌ™

RETRO SPECTŌ™

RETRO SPECTŌ™

RETRO SPECTŌ™

RETRO SPECTŌ™

RETRO SPECTŌ™

RETRO SPECTŌ™

RETRO SPECTŌ™

RETRO SPECTŌ™

RETRO SPECTŌ™

RETRO SPECTŌ™

RETRO SPECTŌ™

RETRO SPECTŌ™

RETRO SPECTŌ™

effort, services	deputy, lieutenant	number
moon	luxury, extravagance	memory
door	tear	letter
shape, beauty	thanks	hour
flame	her (accusative case)	him (accusative case)

RETRO Specto™

RETRO Specto™

RETRO Specto™

RETRO Specto™

RETRO Specto™

RETRO Specto™

RETRO Specto™

RETRO Specto™

RETRO Specto™

RETRO Specto™

RETRO Specto™

RETRO Specto™

RETRO Specto™

RETRO Specto™

RETRO Specto™

latrō, latrōnis (m)	eques, equitis (m)	mors, mortis (f)
sanguis, sanguinis (m)	aetās, aetātis (f)	crēdō, crēdere, crēdidī, crēditum
dūcō, dūcere, dūxī, ductum	avis, avis (f,i)	homō, hominis (m)
imāgō, imaginis (f)	magnitūdō, magnitūdinis (f)	multitūdō, multitūdinis (f)
pēs, pedis (m)	dīco, dīcere, dīxī, dictum	vīvō, vīvere, vīxī, vīctum

injury, injustice	nature, birth	star
middle	measure, mode	to ask or question
to drive, stir up, agitate	to order or command	to help or manage
to name, mention, call by name	trial, legal investigation	duty, respect
zeal, study	wine	fault

sextus, -a, -um	decimus, -a, -um	centum
mille, milia	conservō, conservāre, conservāvī, conservātum	servō, servāre, servāvī, servātum
dēbeō, dēbēre, dēbuī, dēbītum	valeō, valēre, valuī, valītum	pecūnia, -ae
poena, -ae	sententia, -ae	vīta, -ae
sapienta, -ae	culpa, -ae	rīpa, -ae

third	fourth	fifth
nine	ten	first
four	five	seven
one	two	three
arms	battle	sword

RETRO Specтō™

RETRO Specтō™

RETRO Specтō™

RETRO Specтō™

RETRO Specтō™

RETRO Specтō™

RETRO Specтō™

RETRO Specтō™

RETRO Specтō™

RETRO Specтō™

RETRO Specтō™

RETRO Specтō™

RETRO Specтō™

RETRO Specтō™

RETRO Specтō™

somnus, -ae	calculus, -ae	cavus, -ae
respondeō, respondēre, respondī, responsum	rīdeō, rīdēre, rīsī, rīsum	terreō, terrēre, terruī, terrītum
timeō, timēre, timuī	princeps, principis (c)	soror, sorōris (f)
frāter, frātris (m)	māter, mātris (f)	pāter, pātris (m)
parēns, parentis (c, i)	nāvis, nāvis (f, i)	senex, senis (m)

RetroSpectō™

RetroSpectō™
RetroSpectō™
RetroSpectō™
RetroSpectō™
RetroSpectō™
RetroSpectō™
RetroSpectō™
RetroSpectō™
RetroSpectō™
RetroSpectō™
RetroSpectō™
RetroSpectō™
RetroSpectō™
RetroSpectō™

sixth	tenth	hundred
thousand/ thousands	to conserve	to save
to owe	be strong, be well	money
penalty, punishment	sentence	life
wisdom	fault, blame, sin	river bank

MAKE YOUR OWN CARDS!

Notes

Notes

Notes

Notes

Notes

Notes

Notes

Notes

Notes

Notes

Notes

Classical Subjects Creatively Taught™

LATIN Alive! BOOK 1

Karen Moore
Gaylan DuBose

Latin Comes ALIVE!

Latin is an elegant and ancient language that has been studied for many generations. It is also quite alive in our culture and in the languages we speak today. You will be surprised at what you learn in each new chapter of *Latin Alive! Book One*. As the first text in a three-year series, it is a rigorous and thorough introduction to this great language, and is designed to engage the upper school (middle and high school) student. Brimming with relevant facts and stories, this text offers something for everyone.

- 36 weekly chapters, including 29 new content chapters and 7 review "reading" chapters
- Pronunciation guides
- Weekly introduction of vocabulary
- Thorough grammatical explanations, including all five noun declensions and cases, all verb conjugations, irregular verbs, various pronouns, adjectives, and adverbs
- United States state seals and their Latin mottos
- Extensive study of the Latin derivatives of English words
- Substantial Latin readings and translation exercises
- Lessons and stories of Roman culture, myths, and history
- Exercises and questions to prepare students for the National Latin Exam and the Advanced Placement Exam
- Includes historical contributions from Christopher Schlect, historian and academic dean at New Saint Andrews College, Moscow, ID.
- Teacher's Edition, including answer keys, teacher's helps, and additional activities available separately

How does this text compare with *Latin for Children*?
This first text in the *Latin Alive!* series serves as both an introduction for the middle school and high school student who has not previously studied Latin, and also as a "bridge text" into more advanced study for students who have studied Latin in grammar school. If your student has gone through all of the *Latin for Children Primers*, you will find this first year of *Latin Alive!* to be one of accelerated review, with greater explanation of grammar and increased reading and translation.

Get *free* samples, videos, and more on our website: www.ClassicalAcademicPress.com

Learn more than how to order a taco!™

Classical Subjects Creatively *Practiced*

Headventure Land™

www.HeadventureLand.com

A fun **FREE** site to **PRACTICE** your *LFC B* Latin!